Nelson Thornes Shakespeare

Macbeth

TEACHER RESOURCE BOOK

Volume editor: **Dinah Jurksaitis**

Series editors: **Duncan Beal and Dinah Jurksaitis**

Series consultant: **Peter Thomas**

Text © Dinah Jurksaitis 2003

The right of Dinah Jurksaitis to be identified as author of this work has been asserted by her in accordance with the Copyright, Designs and Patents Act 1988.

All rights reserved. The copyright holders authorise ONLY users of *Nelson Thornes Shakespeare: Macbeth Teacher Resource Book* to make photocopies of vi –viii and 1 –79 for their own or their students' immediate use within the teaching context. No other rights are granted without permission in writing from the publishers or under licence from the Copyright Licensing Agency Limited. Further details of such licences (for reprographic reproduction) may be obtained from the Copyright Licensing Agency Limited, of 90 Tottenham Court Road, London W1T 4LP.

Copy by any other means or for any other purpose is strictly prohibited without prior written consent from the copyright holders. Application for such permission should be addressed to the publishers.

Any person who commits any unauthorised act in relation to this publication may be liable to criminal prosecution and civil claims for damages.

Published in 2003 by:
Nelson Thornes Ltd
Delta Place
27 Bath Road
CHELTENHAM
GL53 7TH
United Kingdom

03 04 05 06 07 / 10 9 8 7 6 5 4 3 2 1

A catalogue record for this book is available from the British Library

ISBN 0 7487 6961 7

Page make-up by Tech Set

Printed in Croatia by Zrinski

Acknowledgements

Associated Press: p65; Mary Evans Picture Library: p9, p13, p18, p19, p29, p31, p35, p38, p42, p45, p46, p49; Shakespeare Birthplace Trust: p20; Werner Forman: p4

Contents

Introduction		v
Shakespeare and GCSE English		vi
Shakespeare and GCSE English Literature		vii
Shakespeare and AS English Literature		viii

Student Activities

1	Fair is foul and foul is fair	1
2	The battle	2
3	Imagery: simile	3
4	Performance interpretation: witches (1)	4
5	Blank verse (1)	5
6	Blank verse (2)	6
7	Clothing imagery	8
8	Echoing...choing...oing...ing...g	9
9	Dramatic irony and diplomatic talk	10
10	Night and day	11
11	Lady Macbeth	12
12	Contrast and double	14
13	Soliloquy and watching Shakespeare's language	15
14	Relationship and euphemism	16
15	Sound and guilt	17
16	Washing	18
17	Descent into hell	19
18	The Porter's speech	20
19	Equivocation	22
20	Equivocation in Act 2 Scene 3	23
21	The media roll in	25
22	Performance interpretation: place	26
23	Obsession: a close study	27
24	How things have changed!	28
25	Sleep and nightmares	29
26	Compare with the murder of Duncan	30
27	Performance interpretation: the ghost	31
28	Things change	33
29	Dissidents	34
30	Performance interpretation: witches (2)	36
31	Spells and visions	38
32	Coded language	39
33	Birds	41
34	The slaughter of the innocents	42
35	Good king, bad king	43
36	The king's touch	45
37	Bad news	47
38	Sleep-walking and sleep-talking	48
39	Blank verse (3): *tomorrow and tomorrow*	50

End of Play Activities

40	Your own blank verse speeches	52
41	Character collage, programme notes, modern version	53
42	Alternative views	55
43	Uses and abuses of the text	56

Character Sheets

44–7	Macbeth	57–60
48–9	Banquo	61–2
50–1	Duncan	63–4
52–4	Lady Macbeth	65–7

Coursework Assignments

Coursework Assignment 1 (GCSE)	68
Coursework Assignment 2 (GCSE)	70
Coursework Assignment 3 (GCSE)	72
Coursework Assignment 4 (GCSE)	74
Coursework Assignment 5 (AS)	76
Coursework Assignment 6 (AS)	78

Activity Grids

Student activities grouped according to subject areas

Subject	Activity Sheet Numbers
Performance	4, 21, 22, 27, 30, 41
Dramatic technique	9, 12, 13, 17, 18, 35
Language	2, 3, 5, 6, 7, 8, 9, 14, 19, 20, 32, 39, 40, 42
Reading only	10, 19
Background contexts	8, 16, 20, 29, 31, 32, 33, 34, 36

Specific to character
  Macbeth
  Lady Macbeth
  Banquo
  Duncan
	
	7, 23, 25, 26, 44–7
	11, 14, 28, 34, 38, 52–4
	48–9
	50–1

Student activities particularly appropriate for suggested coursework assignments

GCSE

Assignment 1	7, 23, 25, 26, 44–7
Assignment 2	11, 14, 28, 38, 52–4
Assignment 3	4, 8, 16, 25, 27, 30, 31
Assignment 4	7, 9, 10, 12, 18, 19, 20, 38

AS LEVEL

Assignment 5	1, 3, 9, 12, 19, 20, 26, 32, 35
Assignment 6	9, 11, 12, 14, 23, 34, 36, 37, 38, 39

Introduction

To the teacher

Within the **student editions** you will find:
- **introductory essays** concerned with the play's cultural context, or literary sources
- **introductions** to each scene
- **line by line notes** on vocabulary and idiom
- **explanations of interesting points** of language and versification, such as imagery, wordplay, verse and prose
- **performance features** – often one per page – inviting students to consider the play in performance: the possibilities of character presentation, of action, and of mood.
- **comparison features** at the end of each scene providing a cross-reference with related scenes and threads. The student's experience of the play is often disjointed, spread over a series of lessons, so this feature helps to see how a scene fits the wider picture
- **scene summaries** at the end of each scene.

In this **Resource Book** you will find challenging activities to complement a reading of the play.
- **Scene by scene worksheets** are designed to help students think about the events of a scene in the context of the whole play. Most worksheets comprise clear tasks, such as a search for evidence to support a view of a character. Some are more explanatory, developing a language point. These sheets are suitable for both writing and discussion. They are particularly useful for helping an absentee student catch up on missed scenes.
- **Character Sheets** allow students to see how our view of a character develops over the course of the play. At key moments students are prompted to add to the summary Character Sheets. They help students to reflect on events and to see how parts relate to the whole.
- A series of **Coursework Assignment** essay titles suggests areas for written response. The teacher can select one before the class begins to study the play. At the end of each Act students consider how the events of that Act contribute towards that assignment. By the time they have read the play students will have the understanding and reference necessary to respond to a demanding task.
- At least one of the assignment essay titles addresses the play in performance, providing students with an opportunity to consider different social and historical settings and interpretations. This encourages students to see the play not as a historical relic, but to appreciate the way it spans the centuries.

Our aim is to provide a resource for teachers which recognises the problems of school-based Shakespeare: a play written to be performed, but largely experienced as a text to be read in a class; a play often read with specific ends in mind depending on the syllabus followed. We hope that this Resource Book will offer support to the teacher faced with this rewarding challenge.

Duncan Beal and Dinah Jurksaitis

Shakespeare and GCSE English

Listed below are descriptions of the criteria for gaining a grade C and a grade A at GCSE level.

Criteria for personal response to Shakespeare

General criteria for gaining a grade C

Candidates give a personal and critical response to literary texts which show understanding of the ways in which meaning is conveyed. They refer to aspects of language, structure and themes to support their views.

Specific criteria for gaining a grade C in response to Shakespeare

Candidates show insight when discussing
- the nature of the play, its implications and relevance
- characters, structure and stagecraft
- Shakespeare's use of language.

General criteria for gaining a grade A

Candidates appreciate and analyse alternative interpretations, making cross references where appropriate. They develop their ideas and refer in detail to aspects of language, structure and presentation, making apt and careful comparison within and between texts.

Specific criteria for gaining a grade A in response to Shakespeare

Candidates show analytical and interpretative skills when evaluating
- the play's moral and philosophical context
- significant achievements within the dramatic genre
- Shakespeare's exploitation of language for dramatic, poetic and figurative effect.

Shakespeare and GCSE English Literature

Listed below are descriptions of the criteria for gaining a grade C and a grade A at GCSE level.

Criteria for personal response to Shakespeare

General criteria for gaining a grade C

Candidates demonstrate insight into how different meanings and ideas are conveyed through language, structure and form. They explore connections and comparisons between texts, referring to details to support their views. They convey their ideas and responses in an appropriate range of exploratory forms. They show insight when discussing the social and historical settings of the texts, their cultural contexts or the literary traditions on which they draw.

Specific criteria for gaining a grade C in response to Shakespeare

Candidates show insight when discussing
- character and action
- the effects of dramatic devices or structures
- language, ideas and themes
- the text's setting or cultural context or tradition.

General criteria for gaining a grade A

Candidates respond critically and sensitively to texts, exploring alternative approaches and interpretations. They consider and evaluate the ways meaning, ideas and feelings are conveyed through language, structure and form. They respond in appropriate forms, conveying their ideas coherently, vigorously and persuasively. They show analytical and interpretative skills when evaluating the social and historical settings of texts, their cultural contexts or the literary traditions on which they draw.

Specific criteria for gaining a grade A in response to Shakespeare

Candidates show analytical and interpretative skills when evaluating
- the effects of character and action
- the effects of dramatic devices or structures
- the layers of meaning in language, ideas and themes
- the social and historical setting or cultural context or literary tradition.

Shakespeare and AS English Literature

Listed below is a useful summary of the Assessment Objectives at this level, together with the criteria for personal response to Shakespeare.

Note: An examination board that does not specify a particular Assessment Objective in relation to the study of Shakespeare or a particular Criterion in relation to response to Shakespeare is given in [square brackets].

1 Assessment Objectives for the study of Shakespeare

Candidates are required to demonstrate their ability to:

- communicate clearly the knowledge, understanding and insight appropriate to literary study, using appropriate terminology and accurate and coherent written expression;
- respond with knowledge and understanding to literary texts of different types and periods; [not OCR]
- show detailed understanding of the ways in which writers' choices of form, structure and language shape meanings; [not AQA B]
- articulate independent opinions and judgements, informed by different interpretations of literary texts by other readers;
- show understanding of the contexts in which literary texts are written and understood. [not AQA A]

2 Criteria for personal response to Shakespeare

- Knowledge and understanding of the nature of literary study; effective use of literary terms; accurate and fluent written expression; clear argument with textual reference.
- Engagement with the play and its literary features; knowledge and understanding of the play; examination of period and generic features. [not OCR]
- Features of language, form and structure; their effects; and contribution to meaning. [not AQA B]
- Personal response and argument; understanding of differing critical approaches; exploration of the play's meaning.
- Exploration of context; its connections with the play; and its effects on responses to the play. [not AQA A]

Act 1: Scene 1 *Student Activities* **1**

Fair is foul and foul is fair

A major theme in *Macbeth* is that things can be understood in opposite ways. For example, a hero who kills in war could kill in peacetime. A country which wins a war may have lost also because it cost so much life and money. On the other hand, every cloud has a silver lining. So what seems bad is often good.

Antithesis

There are many antitheses in *Macbeth*.

lost	won
fair	foul
comfort	discomfort
live	die
heaven	Hell
lies	truth
night	day

> **Antithesis** is the **direct opposite** or **complete contrast**.

With a partner choose one of the above pairs of words.

Choose one word each.

Each of you arrange your partner's body into a statue that gives an image of his/her word.

Demonstrate to the rest of the group your joint statue of opposites.

Then:

Think of a short sentence which clearly demonstrates one word.

Think of a sentence of similar length which demonstrates its opposite.

Speak them out loud in sequence.

Here are some examples of **complete contrasts** which come up later in the play:

> angels.........Damnation *(Act 1 Scene 7, lines 19–20)*

> **What hath quench'd them hath given me fire** *(Act 2 Scene 2, line 2)*

> **keep the natural ruby of your cheeks,**
> **When mine is blanch'd with fear.** *(Act 3 Scene 3, lines 14–15)*

Act 1: Scene 2   *Student Activities* **2**

The battle

The audience and the king hear how the battle swung from foul to fair, from bad to good. Two people tell the stories.

 **Interpretation**

Fill in short summaries of what happened. The first two have been done for you.

(Lines 9–15) **FOUL**   *The rebel Macdonwald, with the help of mercenary soldiers, was winning.*

(Lines 15–23) **FAIR**   *Macbeth ripped open the rebel's body from his navel to his neck and cut off his head. The mercenaries ran away.*

(Lines 28–33) **FOUL**

(Lines 35–41) **FAIR**

(Lines 50–4) **FOUL**

(Lines 55–9) **FAIR**

Act 1: Scene 2   Student Activities **3**

Imagery: simile

The Captain fills his story with visual detail using simile to describe what happened in the battle and show how he felt.

> **Simile** is a comparison between two things, using the words *as* or *like*.

Language Discussion

(Lines 8–9)   **As two spent swimmers ... their art**
What are the swimmers doing?
How does this mental picture fit the positions of the two armies in the battle?
Why is the word **choke** a good choice for both battle and swimmers?

(Lines 14–15)   **And Fortune ... like a rebel's whore**
What do a whore and Fortune (or Good Luck) have in common?
How does the comparison fit this particular battle?
How does Macbeth treat this whore (*line 17*)?

(Lines 25–8)   **As whence the sun ... break**
So from that spring ... Discomfort swells
Bad storms come up from the horizon, where the good sun also rises.
What is he saying about the events of the battle in this comparison?
How does this fit the idea of foul and fair?

(Line 35)   **As sparrows eagles, or the hare the lion**
Who are like sparrows and the hare?
Who are like eagles and the lion?

(Line 37)   **As cannons ... cracks**
What does this comparison tell you of the sound and action connected with the two heroes?

Language

Draw a series of quick pictures to illustrate the five similes in the speech.

Character

Describe your impression of the Captain's feelings and experiences.

Act 1: Scene 3 — Student Activities 4

Performance interpretation: witches (1)

Although the witches have a huge influence in the play, they are seen at only two points; at the beginning and in this scene, and then again at the end of Act 3 and the beginning of Act 4. But if you ask anyone what first springs to mind about *Macbeth* they will say 'Witches', because these beings have such a powerful dramatic and thematic impact.

There have been many different ways of interpreting them on stage and film. They represent the influences on us of superstitious powers and evil imagining. Here are some suggestions of how they could be presented:

- in a fortune-teller's tent
- on a tarot telephone line
- in a hall of mirrors, where Macbeth sees his own image in a distorted reflection
- as a nightmare, with voices and a bed shaking
- as a genie coming out of a bottle of gin or beer
- as moving shadows by a fireside or over a bonfire
- as people on the back seat of a bus or pushing past on a train
- as sheep or foxes on a moor, or pigeons in a city square
- as voices over a car radio
- as harpies (bird-like flying spirits with women's faces).

Staging

Either fill out one of these ideas by describing how you would interpret them on stage or in a film. How would you make the voices sound? Some of the words could be written, for example, on a poster in the street or as newspaper headlines.

Or think of another way of portraying them and describe it giving details of how you would make it work for a performance.

Greek vase showing Odysseus with the Sirens.

 **Discussion**

What are your experiences of attempts to foretell the future? Do you think it is possible?

Act 1: Scene 3   Student Activities 5

Blank verse (1)

Read lines 38–41.

At this point in this scene, there is a switch from a 4-beat line of verse, which is the way the witches speak, to a 5-beat line of verse, which is the rhythm of most of the play. The first pentameter (5-beat) line in this scene is Macbeth's first line in the play:

> **So foul and fair a day I have not seen** (line 38)

It is a straightforward example of a line of **blank verse**, which is the verse mostly used in Shakespeare's plays.

Blank verse has a 5-beat line, often with ten syllables (sometimes eleven or nine) and it does not rhyme. That is why it is called blank. The 5 beats in the above line are the words that are stressed when the line is spoken. They have a regular te-tum rhythm like a heart beat.

> So **foul** and **fair** a **day** I **have** not **seen**

Te-tum te-tum te-tum te-tum te-tum (5 main beats)

Banquo then continues in blank verse with these lines:

> How **far** is't **called** to **Forres**? **What** are **these**,
> So **with**ered **and** so **wild** in **their** attire,
> That **look** not **like** th'in**hab**itants **o'** th' **earth** (lines 39–41)

Speak the above lines aloud. Clap on all the stressed beats; that is, on all the words, or parts of words, in bold type.

This is obviously not the way to speak the lines. They are far better given the natural rhythms of ordinary speech; but if you understand the rhythm in the lines, and can hear it clearly even in complicated blank verse, then the poetry can be enriched for both readers and listeners.

Make up a conversation in twos or threes, about ordinary everyday things, in blank verse.

Here is a starter: 'What did you do on Friday afternoon?'
'I went down to the shops to meet a friend.'
'I had a match on Saturday. We won.'
'I had a party at Melissa's house.'
'I had to go and feed my Grandad's dogs.
He's gone away and left me with the job.'

Write down your conversation and highlight the regular 5 stressed beats in each line.

Act 1: Scene 3   Student Activities

Blank verse (2)

Read lines 42–7.

The beats in the next few lines of Banquo's speech are a bit more difficult to hear as they are more subtly used:

> And **yet** are **on** 't? **Live** you? Or **are** you **aught**
> That **man** may **ques**tion? You **seem** to un**der**stand me *(lines 42–3)*

In these lines the beat is not a regular te-tum as before.
- **Live** and **seem** need to be stressed to make the meaning of the lines clear.
- **Live** is stressed before **you** in line 42.
- **seem** is stressed after **You** in line 43.
- If **You** is stressed (and you probably are by now), the sound would keep up the regular te-tum pattern, and the line would sound unnatural and wrong, like this:

> That **man** may **ques**tion? **You** seem **to** under**stand** me

A speaker needs to find the 5 beats in the line which suit the sense best.

If you look at the printed versions of Shakespeare's plays, you can easily identify verse lines because they begin with a capital letter and are in an obvious pattern on the page. However, if you do not have this help, and if you simply listen to the words, the rhythm can be difficult to hear.

Here is a piece of blank verse typed as prose.
Read it aloud and decide where you think the line endings should come. There are seven lines.

> But I must also feel it as a man: I cannot but remember such things were that were most precious to me. Did heaven look on, and would not take their part? Sinful Macduff, they were all struck for thee. Naught that I am, not for their own demerits, but for mine, fell slaughter on their souls. Heaven rest them now.

Now highlight the words, or parts of words, you think should be stressed so as to have 5 beats in a line.

Act 1: Scene 3

 **Language**

Here are Banquo's and Macbeth's next lines in this scene:

Banquo:	By each at once her choppy finger laying
	Upon her skinny lips. You should be women,
	And yet your beards forbid me to interpret
	That you are so.
Macbeth:	Speak if you can. What are you? *(lines 44–7)*

Notice that the last line is divided between the two speakers. That is why Macbeth's speech starts halfway across the page. It is completing Banquo's line.

Highlight the words, or parts of words, which are the beats in the line. Remember 5 beats to each line.

Act 1: Scene 3   *Student Activities* **7**

Clothing imagery

Macbeth has to change from battle behaviour to civilian behaviour. He finds this difficult. He brings his murderous ideas from war into peace. He has just **unseamed** or unstitched the rebel Macdonwald. He should now change from his armour and sword and put on the new clothes of peace.

However, because of his success in battle, he is willing to try on the clothes the witches offer him of being King of Scotland. After all, he has just saved Scotland from enemy and rebel attack. Why shouldn't he be dressed in a king's clothes?

Metaphor

> **Metaphor** is when something is described **as if it is** something else.

In this scene, Macbeth's thoughts are described as though they were bodies that could be dressed in new clothes. He is thinking about being a king, although he is not king; he is trying on the new garments that he would like to have.

Metaphors of clothing are frequent in the play. In this scene alone, there are the following:

Read lines 57 and 142. Macbeth is **rapt**. This word sounds like another word, 'wrapped'. He has clothed himself in a fantasy of being king and is being cloaked or secretive about it.

> **Why do you dress me
> In borrow'd robes?** *(lines 108–9)*

Macbeth is not yet Thane of Cawdor. These clothes do not belong to him.

> **strange garments, cleave not to their mould** *(line 145)*

Banquo uses a clothing metaphor to explain Macbeth's strange mood. New clothes feel odd.

It is possible to show a metaphor dramatically.
How could the witches use a coat or hat when they dress Macbeth in **borrow'd robes**?
How could Duncan use clothing in the scene before this?
Are there any other ways you could use clothing to show ideas so far in the play?

How do metaphors of clothing add to your understanding of things changing or not being what they seem?

 **Discussion**

How are the clothes we wear today indicative of our status or social group?

Stealth bombers and cloaking devices (for avoiding detection by radar) are used in war today. How is deception important in war?

Act 1: Scenes 1, 2, 3   Student Activities **8**

Echoing ... choing ... oing ... ing ... g

Hover through the fog and filthy air *(Act 1 Scene 1, line 12)*

Storm, on land and sea, echoes through the first three scenes in sound and image.

 **Interpretation**

Scene 1

thunder, lightning ... rain *(line 2)*

Scene 2

Find quotations that show storms.

Scene 3

Witches were popularly believed to create storms, thrive on chaos and sail in sieves.

Agnis Tompson confessed that, with two hundred other witches,
'all they together went to Sea, each one in a riddle or cive [sieve], and went into the same very substantially, with flaggons of wine, making merry and drinking by the way in the same riddles ir cives, to the Kirke [church] of North Barrick in Lowthian'.

What do the witches plan to do to the master of the *Tiger*?

Find Macbeth's first words in this scene.

Find the first two words of each of the witches in this scene:

1st witch: _____   2nd witch: _____   3rd witch: _____

All hail means 'Greetings' but there is an echo of hailstorms.

In Macbeth's soliloquy *(lines 130–47)* the idea of chaos in nature is continued. Find quotations to show this.

A sorcerer selling wind tied in knots to sailors.

Act 1: Scene 4 Student Activities 9

Dramatic irony and diplomatic talk

Duncan welcomes Macbeth and Banquo, victorious from battle. The scene follows straight after we have heard Macbeth's fantasies about killing Duncan, so the audience knows what is going on in Macbeth's thoughts but Duncan does not.

Dramatic irony

Duncan is speaking of the Thane of Cawdor in a way that is heard by the audience as appropriate for Macbeth. Duncan himself is not aware how appropriate it is.

> **Dramatic irony** is when an audience knows something that some or all of the characters on stage do not know. Words are then spoken which mean different things to the audience and to the unsuspecting characters.

How are the following ironic?
- Duncan's speech followed by Macbeth's immediate entry
- Macbeth's reply to him

Diplomatic talk

Perhaps, however, Duncan does suspect Macbeth's thoughts. Macbeth could well imagine he had a right to the throne after what he has just achieved, and he is of royal blood. Duncan's welcome of him is not as warm as it could be, and his words are by no means straightforward. In a roundabout way, he could be telling Macbeth not to have any hopes of becoming king.

... would thou hadst less deserv'd *(line 18)* – I wish you had deserved less payment.

More is thy due than more than all can pay *(line 21)* – You have deserved more than I can possibly pay you, because I do not intend to pay you **all** (ie the crown).

Duncan's words sound like an elaborate compliment but they could hide his fear of what Macbeth may be hoping. The fact that he makes his own son, Malcolm, heir to the throne immediately afterwards is significant.

Either improvise in groups of four:
- one read Duncan's lines
- one speak his thoughts straight afterwards
- one reply with Macbeth's lines
- one speak his thoughts straight afterwards

Or, individually, write and draw this as a cartoon, with spoken words and 'thinks' bubbles.

Explain how in this scene foul is fair.

Act 1: Scene 5

Night and day

Student Activities **10**

This is a reading sheet only

The issue of night and day is an important topic and is developed later in the play.

In Act 1 Scene 3, the witches chant their curse on the pilot:

> **Sleep shall neither night nor day**
> **Hang upon his penthouse lid** *(lines 19–20)*

Night and Day, Dark and Light are confused from the start, when the day is foggy and filthy.

In Act 1 Scene 4, Macbeth prays:

> **Stars, hide your fires!**
> **Let not light see my black and deep desires** *(line 50)*

Light reminds him of his conscience. He wishes night's lights were out.

In Act 1 Scene 5, Lady Macbeth prays:

> **Come, thick Night,**
> **And pall thee in the dunnest smoke of Hell,**
> **That my keen knife see not the wound it makes,**
> **Nor Heaven peep through the blanket of the dark,**
> **To cry, 'Hold, hold!'** *(lines 49–53)*

Again, exactly like her husband, she prays that the powers of good, represented by light, may not see her evil. Her prayer is particularly poignant as she uses the word **blanket**, which sounds homely and domestic.

At the end of this scene, she is determined that Duncan shall not leave their house alive.

> **O, never**
> **Shall sun that morrow see!** *(lines 59–60)*

But, as the play shows later, the light goes out of her life and out of Macbeth's life on the next day. Also, later, neither she nor Macbeth can sleep, which further confuses Night with Day.

This confusion emphasises the connection between Macbeth, Lady Macbeth and the witches. Witches perform their activities mostly at night, or, if not then, in the thickest darkness and fogs of day, when according to James I in *Daemonologie*, his book on witches, the devil is able to

> thicken and obscure so the air that is next about them
> ... that the beams of any other man's eye cannot pierce
> through the same to see them.

It was also thought that witches needed thick, dark air in order to fly. If they needed this in daytime then the devil would thicken the air for them. So Lady Macbeth and Macbeth both ask for light to be thickened or stars to be put out.

There are many more references to Night and Day, Dark and Light, in the play as it proceeds.

Act 1: Scene 5

Student Activities 11

Lady Macbeth

In a preface to his *Chronicles of Scotland,* Holinshed describes the women of Scotland at the time of Macbeth. This quotation may give some light on how Shakespeare saw the character of Lady Macbeth.

> **In these daies also the women of our countries were of no less courage than the men: for all stout maidens and wives ... marched as well in the field as did the men and so soone as the armie did set forward, they sleue the first living creature that they found, in whose bloud they not onelie bathed their swords, but also tasted thereof with their mouthes.**

In the play there are a number of important points at which we get insights into Lady Macbeth's character.

The letter
- This is Lady Macbeth's first appearance in the play.
- Her first words are not her own. They are the witches' and Macbeth's.
- The letter tells us a lot about her husband's feelings for her.

Her own first words:
- echo the witches' words
- show her determination
- show her knowledge of her husband
- tell how she plans to persuade him to go for the crown.

Look at her experience. First she hears the prophecy and then the messenger.
- She hears the witches' prophecy.
- She fantasises about future evil actions to bring it about.
- She suddenly discovers it could possibly be true.
- This follows the pattern of Macbeth's experience.

Her prayer to evil spirits is:
- a reversal of a prayer for good
- a reversal of fruitful womanhood
- a reversal of light.

When she greets her husband, she:
- shows her feelings for him and for his news
- immediately starts to use her influence with him.

Act 1: Scene 5   *Student Activities 11,* continued

Fair is foul. Her advice to him is:

- to **look like the innocent flower, / But be the serpent under't** (lines 64–5)

The devil took the shape of a snake to tempt Eve to eat the apple in the Garden of Eden.

Adam and Eve in the Garden of Eden with the devil as a serpent under the tree.

Hot seat

Imagine you are, or a member of your group is, the messenger. Question him. For example: 'How did Lady Macbeth react to your news?'; 'What did she look like?'; 'What do you think the letter in her hand said?'

Essay

This is Lady Macbeth's first appearance in the play. She makes a very quick and forceful impact. Referring to this scene only, describe your impression of her.

Act 1: Scene 6 — Student Activities 12

Contrast and double

Contrast

Drama depends on *contrast*.
Macbeth is about antithesis and two sides to things.

Structure

How does this scene, in the first ten lines, contrast sharply with the previous scene? Find at least four contrasts.

Think about these words: birds, heaven, cradle, sweet. Find contrasting words from the previous scene.

Double

Re-read the conversation between Lady Macbeth and Duncan. Who is being *double*?

Character

In groups of four:
- one read Lady Macbeth's words
- one speak Lady Macbeth's thoughts straight afterwards
- one read Duncan's words
- one speak Duncan's thoughts straight afterwards.

Now present the scene as a mime.

Why is Macbeth not here to greet his guests?

Character

Choose one of the following imagined situations and improvise Macbeth's words.
- Macbeth has escaped to the stable to avoid having to meet Duncan. He is grooming his horse and is talking to him/her.
- Macbeth is standing in front of his wardrobe wondering what to wear for the welcoming feast. What will hide his thoughts best, he asks himself.
- Macbeth is getting washed before the guests arrive. He looks in the mirror and shaves himself. What is he thinking?
- Macbeth is in the kitchens of the castle watching the cooks prepare for the evening feast. He tastes some of the dishes. Improvise his thoughts.

Act 1: Scene 7   Student Activities *13*

Soliloquy and watching Shakespeare's language

Soliloquy

Macbeth is tortured by his evil thoughts. An audience often hears his conscience and his private thoughts in the play. His first soliloquy is in Act 1 Scene 3, lines 130–47. Scene 7 opens with his second soliloquy (lines 1–28).

> A **soliloquy** is the speech of a character who is talking on stage as if to himself/herself. Thoughts are spoken out loud, but no one else on stage can hear them. The character may also be alone. The audience can hear, but is not being directly addressed.

What are Macbeth's worries about killing Duncan?

Watching Shakespeare's language

Imagine you are making a film of *Macbeth*. As he speaks his soliloquy in this scene, instead of showing the man, show visual interpretations of the images that he uses. His mind leaps across a whole range of pictures.

Divide the 28 lines into seven or eight images, which a film camera could pan over as Macbeth speaks the words. One idea is suggested here for the first image:

Pick out the words **catch** (line 3) and **bank and shoal** (line 6).

The camera shows a fishing net being pulled up onto a sandy beach. In it, tangled with seaweed, is a crown.

Either use this idea **or** find another one for these lines.

Now continue, picking out the words which inspire the image, and describing how you have decided to show them.

Write/improvise a soliloquy for Banquo at this point in the play. He is at table with the king. Macbeth, who seems disturbed, has left the room. Banquo is watching Lady Macbeth.

Act 1: Scene 7 — Student Activities 14

Relationship and euphemism

From this time
Such I account thy love *(lines 38–9)*

In Holinshed's *Chronicles of Scotland*, we see that Shakespeare has combined the stories of two traitors in Scotland: Donwald and Makbeth. Interestingly, their relationships with their two wives have something in common also.

Donwald, 'kindled in wrath by the words of his wife, determined to follow her advice in the execution of so heinous an act'.

Makbeth considered murder because 'specially his wife lay sore upon him … as she was very ambitious'.

 **Discussion**

From her entrance *(line 28)*, to the end of the act, how does Lady Macbeth persuade her husband to agree to the murder of Duncan? Where does she:
- question his love for her?
- question his courage?
- question if he is a man?
- compare him with herself?
- suggest practical ways to do the murder?
- describe how she will pretend to be innocent?

Euphemism

Neither Macbeth nor Lady Macbeth mentions the word 'murder'. They avoid it.

> A **euphemism** describes a less unpleasant word for an unpleasant thing

List any euphemisms you find in this scene.

 **Discussion**

Macbeth echoes Lady Macbeth's ideas. The rhyming couplet at the end of the act sounds decisive:

> **Away, and mock the time with fairest show:**
> **False face must hide what the false heart doth know.** *(lines 82–3)*

Do you think Macbeth wants to kill Duncan all along, but needs his wife to persuade him, so that he does not feel that he is responsible himself? Can you justify this point of view?

Act 2: Scene 2 Student Activities **15**

Sound and guilt

Sound

 Interpretation

Make a list of the sounds mentioned in this scene. Start with the end of the previous scene.

- *A bell rings.*
-
-
-
-
-
-
-
-
-

The scene is 'framed' by sound, from the bell to the knocking. Creatures and voices are heard. The peace of sleep and quiet conscience is attacked.

How is sound important in this scene?

Guilt

We speak about having a **quiet conscience**.
All the guests and servants in the castle are asleep.
Macbeth murders Duncan while he is asleep.
Macbeth murders his own quiet.

How does Macbeth describe **sleep** *(lines 35–9)*?
What could the knocking represent?

Act 2: Scene 2   Student Activities 16

Washing

Water and washing are important in many cultures and religions. Often washing has become a ritual.

 **Discussion**

Do you know of any rituals that are connected with washing?

A Russian Orthodox baptism.

In the Christian religion, water washes away sin and shows the beginning of a pure new life.

People are baptised with the sign of a cross, made in water, on the forehead. Sometimes adults are completely submerged in water, perhaps in a river, when they take on a new life in this religion.

In some of Shakespeare's other plays, the sea is a symbol of a fresh start: for example, in *Hamlet*, *The Winter's Tale*, *Twelfth Night* and *The Tempest*.

Water indicates that evil is being cleaned away. Sins are forgiven.

In classical mythology, there is a river, Lethe, at the entrance to the underworld (the space between earth and hell). This is a river of forgetfulness.

Macbeth and Lady Macbeth have different attitudes to washing. Describe what this shows about each one of them. Is it in keeping with what we have already seen of their characters in the play?

Act 2: Scene 2 Student Activities **17**

Descent into hell

In Heaven

In Act 1 Scene 6, Banquo says of Macbeth's castle: **heaven's breath / Smells wooingly here**. *(lines 5–6)*

On Earth

In Act 1 Scene 7, Macbeth describes himself as on Earth, **here, upon this bank and shoal of time**. *(line 6)*

Going to Hell

Here in Scene 2, Macbeth is making his descent to hell. He has committed a foul murder and cannot be forgiven, nor can he ever forget.

Line 16 is laid out almost like a descending staircase:

> **Did not you speak?**
>   **When?**
>   **Now.**
>   **As I descended?** *(line 16)*

In Hell

In the scene following this one, the Porter at Macbeth's castle gate pretends that he is the keeper of hell-gate. **If a man were Porter of Hell Gate, he should have old turning the key.** *(lines 1–2)*

> Medieval plays were performed on carts, often pulled around from town to town. They showed Heaven on the cart, where there were angels, God, and the saints. On the ground in front was Earth, where people acted out their stories, and under the cart was Hell and the devils. Sometimes Earth was acted on the cart also, so that everyone could see the action. The carts on which these plays were performed were called pageants, from which the dramas themselves took their names.

Passion play being performed in a street.

 **Staging**

In groups, make a design for a stage that could show this idea of descent. You could choose a medieval one, or a completely modern one, or a design from any other time, even the future.

Act 2: Scene 3 *Student Activities* **18**

The Porter's speech

Time is needed to allow Macbeth and Lady Macbeth to get ready to appear in public. In addition, it is common in drama to have a comic interlude after the tension of earlier scenes, or before tragedy or powerful feeling in later scenes.

 **Interpretation**

What effect does the Porter's speech have here? Does it:
- get rid of an audience's laughter before the serious discovery later in the scene?
- keep up the suspense by delaying the discovery of the body?

> In medieval mystery plays, the porter at hell-gate was a standard comic character. He made topical and often bawdy jokes, which could be varied for all sorts of reasons, for example:
> - according to the place where the play was performed, so jokes would be about parts of the town, or the mayor, or the local villain or aristocracy;
> - commenting on events of national or general public interest, such as a new law that had been passed, or a discovery that had been made.

This performance suggested the historical times of the play, ie the 11th century. The Porter is lying drunk on the steps.

Act 2: Scene 3

Sometimes, the Porter's speech in *Macbeth* is entirely rewritten in modern English and done as a stand-up comic act with political, local, dirty and other jokes. Some of the following are loosely connected with the Macbeth situation:

- 'I'm so tired!' said the woman to her friend. 'Last night I didn't sleep until after three.' 'No wonder you're tired,' her friend replied. 'Twice is usually all I need.'
- Duncan enters a chemist shop. 'I want a deodorant.'
  'Ball or aerosol,?' asks the chemist.
  'No,' says Duncan, 'armpits.'
- Politicians are a bunch of bananas. They start off green, turn yellow, and there's not a straight one in the bunch.
- Two blokes are standing at the corner of King and Pit Street. First bloke sniffs the air and says, 'You didn't fart just then, did you?' His mate, offended replies, 'Of course I did. You don't think I smell like that all the time do you?'
- Man goes into a bar with his wife and says quickly to the barman,
  'Give me a drink before it starts.' He gets one and drinks it.
  'Give me another one,' he says, 'before it starts.'
  The puzzled barman says, 'There's no show on here tonight, sir. Strippers is Fridays.'
  Again the man says, 'Give us another before it starts.' Then his wife says, 'Haven't you had enough, dear?' Then the man says to the barman,
  'See, it's started!'
- In Heaven, the police are English, the chefs are French, the engineers are German, the managers are Swiss, and the lovers are Italian.
  In Hell, the chefs are English, the police are German, the managers are French, the engineers are Italian and the lovers are Swiss.
- Two women were watching a funeral go by. 'Who died?' said Gloria.
  Her friend replied, 'The poor sod in the back who's lying down.'

 and

Find your own better jokes that relate in some way to the Macbeth situation.

_____
_____
_____
_____
_____
_____
_____

Act 2: Scene 3   Student Activities **19**

Equivocation

This is a reading sheet only

Example 1

A boy is on a bus, right at the front, without a ticket. The boy picks up a ticket from the floor. The conductor comes to get the fare. The boy holds up the ticket. 'Got one', he says. The conductor assumes that it was bought and goes away!

> **Equivocate** To equivocate means to use ambiguous words or expressions in order to mislead.

(The boy did not lie. He spoke the truth but did not explain the full truth. The conductor made an assumption. Equivocation.)

Example 2

You are kidnapped and are asked by the kidnappers if your father has any money. You answer that he owns the clothes he stands up in.

(He does own the clothes he stands up in, but he also owns a personal yacht, which you did not happen to mention. They let you go. Equivocation for a good purpose.)

Example 3

A girl walks out of a shop with a skirt over her arm that she has not paid for. After trying it on she decided she wanted it and then just walked off with it, forgetting to pay. She is caught outside, and comes before the magistrates. She has to say whether she pleads Guilty or Not Guilty. She says, 'I'll plead Guilty, because you won't believe me anyway.'

(This is called an Equivocal Plea and is not allowed by the court because she cannot say she is Guilty and Not Guilty at the same time as they contradict each other.)

 **Equivocation**

The word derives from the Latin Aequi + vocare – to call alike.

- Equivocation is not lying, because the truth is spoken.
- There can often be a regard for the truth, and a concern not to lie.

BUT

- The speaker is aware of what meaning the listener will take from his words. The listeners infer meanings because of the cast of their minds.

AND

- Equivocation is not necessarily evil, and can be for a good purpose. It can also mislead for wrong purposes.

ALSO

- A modern phrase to describe one kind of equivocation is that a person is ECONOMICAL WITH THE TRUTH.

Act 2: Scene 3 — Student Activities 20

Equivocation in Act 2 Scene 3

The Porter introduces this word. Meanwhile Macbeth is changing his clothes and washing his hands to mislead the thanes.

The Porter admits into his Hell,

> **an equivocator, that could swear in both scales against either scale** *(lines 8–9)*

This is someone who misleads a court inquiry. The scales are the scales of justice.

He goes on,

> **who committed treason enough for God's sake** *(line 10)*

This probably refers to Father Garnet, the Catholic priest who was involved with the Gunpowder Plot to kill James I. He committed treason, for what he saw as God's sake. He took part in the plot because he thought James was stopping England from becoming a Catholic country again.

Then he says,

> **yet could not equivocate to heaven: O! Come in, equivocator** *(lines 10–11)*

This could refer to Father Garnet, who was hanged and cannot now deceive heaven, so has come down to hell.

And finally, he gives a comic version of the word:

> **much drink is an equivocator with lechery: it makes him, and it mars him; it sets him on, and it takes him off; it persuades him, and disheartens him; makes him stand to, and not stand to; in conclusion, equivocates him in a sleep, and giving him the lie, leaves him** *(lines 30–5)*

Macbeth enters for the first time in public since the murder. Many of his words are equivocations. He speaks truths but they are completely misleading.

> **The labour we delight in physics pain** *(line 49)*

He makes a generalisation that does not refer to his own feelings but implies that this is how he is feeling now.

> **He does; he did appoint so** *(line 52)*

This is a very clear equivocation. The king certainly did appoint to leave today. Macbeth knows that Lennox will hear it as this. Macbeth also knows that the king will not leave today. Yet this is not a lie. He nearly lies. **He does** on its own, would be a lie.

Act 2: Scene 3

 **Interpretation**

How are Macbeth's words in the following lines equivocations? Give both the meaning he intends people to hear (a) and the meaning he understands himself or that betrays his deepest fears (b).

> **'Twas a rough night** *(line 60)*
>
> Whose **renown** and **grace** are dead? *(lines 89–94)*
>
> Who are **them**? *(line 105)*
>
> for **love** of whom did he kill Duncan? *(lines 108–9)*
>
> **manly readiness**. *(line 131)*

(Line 60) (a) _____

(b) _____

(Lines 89–94) (a) _____

(b) _____

(Line 105) (a) _____

(b) _____

(Lines 108–9) (a) _____

(b) _____

(Lines 131) (a) _____

(b) _____

Act 2: Scene 4 *Student Activities* **21**

The media roll in

Either individually or in pairs, choose a newspaper or TV or radio channel and come along with your notebook, microphone and/or camera to record the first versions of events. Interview as many of the characters as possible. Do not forget that there are many other reporters there.

Write up your report.

If possible include a few incriminating photographs, drawings or cartoons!

Think up a really good title. Puns make an impact and are common in news reporting

This story would, of course, be front-page news or headlines.

These notes should help you.
- The media are there.
- There are interpretations of the event by various newspapers, TV and radio channels, all with different audiences and agendas, probably.
- All these characters have versions of the events of the night of the murder:

    Macbeth

    Lady Macbeth

    Banquo

    Macduff

    Lennox

    Ross

    The Old Man

    Other thanes

    Waiting maids

    Groomsmen

    Food tasters

    Macbeth's faithful army sergeants

    Somebody's kids

    The Porter

    Fleance.

People disagree.
People are proved wrong.
Even the butler is suspected.

Act 1: Scene 5 to Act 2: Scene 4   Student Activities **22**

Performance interpretation: place

From Act 1 Scene 5 through to Act 2 Scene 4, the action of the play takes place in, or just outside, the Macbeths' castle. Public, private and outside spaces are needed.

Act 1 Scenes 1 to 4 are in widely different settings and are strongly contrasting in atmosphere.

Imagine you are preparing a **THEATRE** performance of these seven scenes. What would you use to make a difference in atmosphere between the locations?

First, make a list of the changes you will need from scene to scene. Then:

Either discuss your ideas in groups
or work on them individually.

Either write your performance ideas in full
or plan them in note form with illustrations.

- Would you arrange the scene locations physically in different parts of a room or theatre? Think about using different spaces behind an audience, or on a platform, or in an aisle; outside: through a window or door, in an entrance hall, out on the street.
- Would you use music or other sound to change the atmosphere? What different kinds of music/sound would you use? Music can be live, recorded, synthesised. Sound can be anything.
- Would you accompany the scene with a sensation (such as a blast of wind), or with a smell (such as cooking), or with something to eat? You could pass snacks round the audience to give a cocktail-party feel for the feast scene.
- Would you use lighting? These scenes show night and day, inside and outside.
- Or colour, for costume/lighting/props?
- Would you be very traditional and use a stage with a curtain and backdrops with different scenery painted on them? This can give an effective history or story-book atmosphere. If you choose this, what scenes would the paintings show?
- Would you decide to have some scenes shown on a television screen? Or would some scenes be done only with sound and not be visible to an audience at all?

Act 3: Scene 1   *Student Activities* **23**

Obsession: a close study

 **Interpretation**

Read Macbeth's soliloquy *(lines 47–71)*.

How, in your view, does this speech show Macbeth's obsessions and how does it contribute to our understanding of his degradation?

- Divide the speech up into the following **five** sections.

    From **To be thus** ... *(line 47)* to **To act in safety** *(line 53)*

    From **There is none** ... *(line 53)* to **was by Caesar** *(line 56)*

    From **He chid the Sisters,** ... *(line 53)* to **of mine succeeding** *(line 63)*

    From **If't be so,** ... *(line 63)* to **the seed of Banquo kings!** *(line 69)*

    From **Rather than so** ... *(line 70)* to **Who's there?** *(line 71)*

- Read the speech out loud, changing reader for each section.
  What do you notice about the length of the sentences? Is there a build-up?

- Read the speech again and someone else count the times Macbeth mentions Banquo, either by name, or by using one of the following pronouns: him, he, his, them.

- In pairs, choose one of the following topics. Collect references to them, in the order in which they are referred to in the speech:

  Religion   **Children**   **The throne**   **Murder**

- Report back your findings to the whole group.

- Listen to the sound of lines 63–4. Count how many 's' sounds there are. They could give the effect of Macbeth hissing. Find other lines or parts of lines where sound adds to the sense of what Macbeth is feeling.

- Sometimes the rhythm of the words gives an effect. **Stick deep**, for example, can sound like a dagger thrust. Find any other part of the speech which can be accompanied by an emphatic action. Try it out.

Prepare the second part of the question and then write your answer.

- Look in this speech for evidence of Macbeth's good qualities: honesty about the virtues of others, a concern for life of the soul, courage in the fight. What else?

- Find evidence of how these qualities are now perverted in him and used for evil purposes.

- What happens just before this speech and what happens just after it? Is Macbeth bent on killing Banquo whatever happens?

Act 3: Scene 1 *Student Activities* **24**

How things have changed!

Shakespeare's source story, Holinshed's *Chronicles of Scotland*, says that Macbeth actually reigned for **17 years** before he was eventually murdered by Macduff. It also says that he ruled very well for **10 years**, without committing any atrocities, apart from the murder of Duncan of course. Holinshed states that he

> **... set his whole intention to mainteine iustice, and to punish all enormities and abuses.**

However, things changed, and his conscience

> **... caused him ever to feare, least he should be served of the same cup as he had administered to his predecessor.**

Shakespeare, because of the needs of a fast-moving drama, decided to shrink the time between Macbeth's coming to the throne and the beginning of atrocities against the thanes. When Act 3 begins, there is a strong sense that very few months have elapsed. Macbeth and Lady Macbeth are now installed in Forres, Duncan's palace. In the first conversation with Banquo, Macbeth refers to the sons of Duncan as though the news of their whereabouts is quite recent. However, things have moved on significantly:

- Banquo knows what he thinks *(line 3)*.
- Macbeth knows how to talk to him *(lines 20–2)*.
- Duncan's sons are not keeping a low profile *(lines 31–2)*.
- Macbeth no longer asks his wife what he should do *(line 43)*.
- His obsessions have grown to large proportions *(lines 47–71)*.
- He is rude and dismissive about other men *(in his talk with the murderers)*.
- He has developed a new decisiveness *(lines 140–1)*.
- He uses the royal plural.

Character

How have things changed? Consider:
- Banquo
- the relationship between Lady Macbeth and her husband
- Macbeth's way of speaking with Banquo
- Macbeth's attitude towards the murderers
- Macbeth's concerns when alone.

Act 3: Scene 2 | *Student Activities* **25**

Sleep and nightmares

> Good things of day begin to droop and drowse,
> While night's black agents to their preys do rouse *(Lines 52–3)*

Evil spirits of night come out and attack their prey, and Banquo and Fleance will be attacked this night. The words **night's black agents** refer to the witches along with other spirits. Macbeth is fully aware of the evil he is doing and how he has fled from good.

Is he himself, however, also a prey of the evil agents of night? He cannot sleep and is kept awake by terrible nightmares. Is he a prey for the witches?

When he asks for night to **Scarf up the tender eye of pitiful day** *(line 47)*, could he also mean that he wishes he could not see his own evil, and would like to just get on with what he has to do without recognising what he has lost?

A nightmare.

He calls up the sounds and powers of night as though he is very familiar with them *(lines 46–50)*, and then, almost magician-like, indicates that his spell has worked, **Light thickens** *(line 50)*.

Character Discussion

What **terrible dreams** do you think **shake** him **nightly**?
- Banquo murdering him?
- Himself murdering Banquo, Fleance or Duncan?
- Witches and their sounds and visions?
- Banquo's children with crowns on their heads?
- His wife telling him he is not a man?
- What else?

Character

Either   Make a tableau (a still, silent scene made by a group of people adopting and holding positions – like a group statue), showing aspects of Macbeth's mind at this point in the play.

           Add a few words, either from the text or of your own, to be called out or whispered by the different people in the tableau.

Or   Make a collage, drawing or painting to represent Macbeth's state of mind at this point in the play.

Nelson Thornes Shakespeare: *Macbeth* © Dinah Jurksaitis, Nelson Thornes Ltd, 2003

Act 3: Scene 3 — *Student Activities* **26**

Compare with the murder of Duncan

 **Structure**

Make a comparison between the two murders under these two headings:

Differences

Similarities

Use the following prompts to help you:
- Who commits the murder?
- Where does it take place?
- At what time roughly does it take place?
- How is feasting associated with it?
- Does the audience see it?
- Does the audience hear it?
- Does the audience hear anything else?
- Do the murderers, in either case, feel happy with their achievement?
- What do the sons do in each case?
- Do other people know about the murders?
- Is light significant in either or both?
- How are the murders made dramatic?
- **I am afraid to think what I have done** *(Act 2 Scene 2, line 51)*
  We have lost / Best half of our affair *(Act 3 Scene 3, lines 20–1)*
  Are the murderers aware of losing their souls?

 **Discussion**

Which is the greater evil: to commit a terrible crime like murder, or to make someone else do it for you?

Act 3: Scene 4   *Student Activities* **27**

Performance interpretation: the ghost

Consider these options:
- Does the audience see the ghost?
- Does anyone else see the ghost?
- Does the ghost touch Macbeth?
- Does the ghost touch anyone else?
- Does the ghost make any sound itself, and if so, can it be heard by Macbeth, others at the feast or only the audience?
- Is there really nothing there and no sound either? Is it all in Macbeth's head?

A draped skeleton.

If the ghost is visible, does it look like:
- Banquo as he lived, with bloody gashes?
- A cloaked or sheeted unidentified body?
- A light image flickering on and off, such as moonlight through a window, or candle/torch flames?
- A hologram image of Banquo?
- Behind a gauze screen, a shadow with an unusually large presence on the stage?
- A slow silent drama, at the side of the stage, of Banquo getting up from the ground and walking slowly towards Macbeth and the table?

If the ghost is not visible, would you:
- Make something on the table begin to shake by itself or move about (magnet under the table!)?
- Make a bottle smash on to the floor (invisible string!)?

Act 3: Scene 4 *Student Activities 27, continued*

- Have the three witches come, unseen by the characters, into the room and one of them put on Banquo's coat and sit on the chair, while the others turn a cross upside down or slowly empty the chalice on the floor?
- Create a feeling of a ghost by sound effect?
- Create a feeling of a ghost by a cold or hot wind through the audience?

Staging

In groups decide:
- on exactly which lines the guests and Lady Macbeth react, and what they do
- whether they are in shocked silence and frozen embarrassment; fussing around Macbeth; whispering suspiciously together; gradually realising; all of these or something else?
- when exactly the ghost arrives and what it does.

Then individually or in groups:

either   photocopy the whole scene and mark directions on it;

or   use sheets of paper to interleave the text and mark directions on them, beside the relevant lines;

or   produce the scene for performance.

Act 3: Scene 4 Student Activities **28**

Things change

Lady Macbeth changes in this scene. The vehemence of her words to Macbeth seems to soften, perhaps as she realises that it is no longer possible to maintain the show of innocence, or as she reacts to his obvious illness. How would you describe her mood, character and behaviour as she speaks each of the following speeches? Fill in the spaces below.

Lines 31–6

Lines 52–7

Lines 59–67

Lines 116–19

Line 126

Line 128

Line 140

We do not see Lady Macbeth again in the play for a long time.

Act 3: Scene 6 Student Activities 29

Dissidents

This scene shows dissatisfaction among the ordinary people of Scotland. Lennox and another lord are dissidents, people who disagree with the system of government of the time and who decide to work actively against it.

 **Context**

Compile and design a flyer that Lennox and the other lord might distribute secretly. Choose details of Macbeth's tyranny from the information in this scene and in the play so far. Present it in a convincing, modern way. You could include a cartoon, or design a dissident website that Lennox immediately sets up when he leaves the banquet.

> In Munich, during the Second World War, a number of Germans formed themselves into a group called the White Rose. Sophie Scholl and Willi Graf were two of the young people involved. They risked their lives running an underground printing press to publicise anti-Nazi ideas. They had secret meetings, dropped flyers and painted graffiti at night. They were caught, imprisoned and executed. There is a good film of this called *Die Weisse Rose*.

 **Context**

Design some graffiti, or posters, to represent the views of those who fear and hate Macbeth (Macdeath?). Give some indication in your designs of the details of his crimes as we hear about them in this scene.

 **Context**

Prepare a radio programme, transmitted from the English court by supporters of Malcolm, giving information on Macbeth's activities. Include a couple of interviews with people who have suffered under his tyranny. Include the views of people who used to support him.

> During the era of the USSR, when the citizens of the Soviet Union could not travel freely and did not have free access to information, a radio station called Radio Free Europe operated from neighbouring countries in minority languages, such as Lithuanian, as well as in majority languages. It was run by the Americans as anti-Communist propaganda. It transmitted programmes giving information and holding discussions on topics that were not publicly acknowledged in the Soviet Union, or giving a different perspective on events there.

Act 3: Scene 6 — Student Activities 29, continued

In 1938, Ukrainian dissidents were harshly treated.

Deliver or write a speech for a secret meeting of dissidents against Macbeth. Include the information about him from this scene. Give outlines of the plot to attack him from England, which we hear about here.

In England, at the time when this play was written, there were dissidents. They were Roman Catholic Christians. The king, James I, was a Protestant Christian. The Catholics were not allowed, in England or Scotland, to practise their faith freely. They were persecuted and huge taxes were demanded of them. This had also been the case under Elizabeth I but things were even worse under James I. It is believed that this is what led to the Gunpowder Plot. There must have been many secret meetings to plan this plot.

Act 4: Scene 1
Student Activities **30**

Performance interpretation: witches (2)

At this later stage in the play, ideas about possible interpretations of the witches can be reviewed. This scene develops the presentation of the witches.

- There are more than just three here.
- Hecate is in some position of authority over them.
- They are involved in brewing a cauldron of ingredients.
- They create magical visions of the future and prophesy with confidence to the expectant Macbeth, who drinks up their every word as truth.
- The truths they speak sometimes echo his thoughts and sometimes add new thoughts.

The play does not introduce the audience to many ordinary people in Scotland. But there are some, and they are memorable. So far in the play, there have been:

- the witches *(Act 1 Scenes 1 and 3, Act 3 Scene 5, Act 4 Scene 1)*
- the porter *(Act 2 Scene 3)*
- the old man *(Act 2 Scene 4)*
- the murderers *(Act 3 Scenes 1 and 3)*
- a captain *(Act 1 Scene 2)*.

The witches are usually interpreted as women. They call each other **Sister** *(Act 1 Scene 3)*, Hecate calls them **beldams** *(Act 3 Scene 5, line 2)*. Banquo seems to be in some doubt: **You should be women / And yet your beards forbid me to interpret / That you are so** *(Act 1 Scene 3, lines 45–7)*.

The porter is usually shown as a man. **If a man were porter of hell-gate** *(Act 2 Scene 3, lines 1–2)* and he discusses sexual capability, or lack of it, with inside knowledge!

In 1606, when the play was first produced, all the actors in the troupe were men. It was considered immodest for women to go on the stage. Could the parts be played by the same three people? There were about eight actors when Shakespeare's company went on tour.

Work in groups, pairs or individually.

How could you interpret the characters listed above to show a connection between them?

- Could the actors double (play 2 parts)?
- Are they connected with nature in any way?
- Are they connected with food or drink?

Act 4: Scene 1   *Student Activities 30, continued*

Then ask yourself:

- Could these people be made funny or sent up in some way? Would it detract from the play's impact if they were?
- From your experience of the play only, do you think Shakespeare thought that the witches were to be taken seriously?
- Could you show them represented as a group of ordinary people, such as beggars or factory workers or teachers? If so, how?

Make your answer to this activity:

either   performance based on just these scenes,

or   a set of sketches, cuttings and notes explaining your interpretation,

or   an essay describing how you see these scenes as working in a production and giving reasons for your thinking.

Act 4: Scene 1   *Student Activities* **31**

Spells and visions

Sigmund Freud wrote about his studies of dreams and their interpretation in his book, *The Interpretation of Dreams* (1901). He showed how the images that we create in our sleep can reveal a huge amount about our lives, obsessions and problems.

Joan of Arc saw visions and heard voices which encouraged her to lead an army against the English in France. Many saints in European culture have seen visions and been inspired to act because of them.

More recently, people have experimented with drugs causing visions and auditory experiences. Carlos Castaneda and Aldous Huxley are two famous writers who have recorded their views on these topics. Hallucinatory drugs have been shown to be used by religious groups from around the world to promote an awareness of the spiritual side of life.

We have also seen the devastating effects street drugs such as heroin and cocaine have on individuals. It is now fully known how addictive these can be and how people who become addicted can no longer function normally and are very unhappy and unfulfilled.

In **Act 4 Scene 1** a potion is being concocted and visions are shown. There is no indication in the text that Macbeth is given any of this potion to drink, or anything to eat or smoke or smell, but this could easily happen in a performance and be part of the interpretation of the scene and the witches' general function. They refer to a number of poisons that go into the mixture, but many of the ingredients are simply specialised parts of ordinary creatures, such as the leg of a lizard or the wing of a baby owl.

 **Discussion**

Find out anything you can about:
- mind-changing prepared drugs
- people who have had visions
- natural herbs or foods which have effects on states of mind.

Give a presentation to the rest of the group on what you have researched.

Does the research you have done change your view of Macbeth and his actions? Whatever view you have, make your case either orally or in writing.

Standing in a magic circle, a magician summons a devil to do his bidding.

Act 4: Scene 2

Student Activities 32

Coded language

Re-read carefully Ross's speech to Lady Macduff *(lines 15–25)* and the accompanying notes, which point out the confusion.

When Macbeth is speaking to his wife about his fears of Macduff *(Act 3 Scene 4, lines 127–31)*, he says he keeps paid servants in all his thanes' households to report back to him. The lack of trust is there on both sides. This leads to terrible nervousness about being overheard to say the wrong thing. Lennox *(Act 3 Scene 6)* speaks in very guarded language: **the right valiant Banquo walked too late** and Ross speaks ambiguously so that his words can be heard to mean opposite things at the same time.

 **Discussion**

Could this speech be read as Shakespeare speaking about the times he lived in throughout his childhood, and more especially, later on, the period of the Gunpowder Plot when he was writing the play? Consider:

- Families in many parts of England, including Warwickshire, had been forced by law to change their allegiance from the Catholic to the Protestant church. They had to profess in public what they did not believe in private. This is what in 1598 Jane Wiseman suffered for refusing to declare herself a Protestant:

> **naked, except for a linen cloth about the lower part of her body, be laid upon the ground, lying directly on her back: and a hollow shall be made under her head and her head placed directly in the same; and upon her body in every part let there be placed as much of stones and iron as she can bear and more ... until she die.**

- Jesuit missionaries from France and Spain were in England at the time and were sheltered by many Catholic families who supported what they were doing. John Gerard, who wrote the above account, also wrote about how he escaped from the Tower of London in 1597:

> **The night came. I begged and bribed my warder to let me visit my fellow-prisoner. I walked across. The warder locked the pair of us in the cell ... we had to cut away with a knife the stone holding the socket of the bolt ... The boat came along ... two men got out with a rope. Following my instructions they fastened it to a stake, and listened to the sound of the iron ball I threw down to them.** *(There follows a description of how they slid down the rope. It sounds very modern because it is translated from Latin.)*

Act 4: Scene 2

- There was a rumour that James I had been stabbed on 22 March 1606, just before the attempt on his life was made in the Houses of Parliament.
- A playwright friend of Shakespeare was imprisoned for mocking a Scottish accent in a play.

There are many examples of political situations where citizens have been forced by law, police or armies to say in public that they agree with ideas they hate in private.

There are many examples in ordinary relationships between people where one person feels forced to say something quite unlike what he/she is thinking or feeling.

All through this play there have been examples of characters saying things they did not believe.

 and

Macbeth has commonly been interpreted as a compliment to James I, and indeed it is so on the surface. Could it, however, be subtly deceptive, pretending it is totally in favour of him? Is Shakespeare equivocating with his audience?

 and

Did Shakespeare think that equivocation was the only way to be an honourable man in 16th-century England?

Act 4: Scene 2

Birds

Macbeth is full of mention of birds: the raven, the wren, the mousing owl, the owlet, the martlet, a falcon, sparrows and eagles, rooks, crows and later geese. They have **emblematic meaning**. This means that different kinds of birds have different symbolic meanings.

- The raven is traditionally associated with death or misfortune.
- The martlet, or house-martin, is said to be a bird of blessing which indicates peace, as it builds its nest in happy homes.
- The wren is a cosy, homely little bird, not at all threatening, partly because of its size.
- On the other hand, the falcon and the eagle are birds of prey with all the aggression that suggests.
- The owl, a bird of night, is associated with mystery and fear.

They are brought into the play at significant moments:

- An owl cries while Macbeth is murdering Duncan and Lady Macbeth hears it and is alarmed *(Act 2 Scene 2, line 15)*.
- The Macbeths' castle is likened before the murder to a loving home where martlets breed *(Act 1 Scene 6, line 6)*.
- Lady Macbeth hears a raven when she first contemplates the murder of Duncan in her castle *(Act 1 Scene 5, line 38)*.
- In this scene, Lady Macduff and her little son speak of themselves as birds. They have been abandoned in their nest and have to fend for themselves.

Here is a quotation from the Bible that may have inspired the idea of using birds to create the sense of vulnerability.

> **Behold the fowls of the air: for they sow not, neither do they reap, nor gather into barns; yet your heavenly Father feedeth them.** *(Matthew 6: 26)*.

Context Discussion

What do you think the regular reference to birds adds to the play? Consider:

- how people have thought of witches
- how people associate birds with spirits and the air
- how birds are mostly wild and very few are farmed
- how birds are part of the natural world
- how birds stand for things or symbolise things.

In classical mythology, the harpies are flying humans and in the story of Odysseus, the sirens tempt the hero away from his proper path.

Act 4: Scene 2

The slaughter of the innocents

 **Structure** and  **Character**

Either discuss in groups or individually make short notes on the following:

Find as many ways as you can to compare Lady Macduff with Lady Macbeth. List them under these headings:

Similarities   Differences

Why do you think Shakespeare included so much for the young son of Macduff to say?
Consider:
- what he talks about
- his feelings about his father
- the way he is killed.

Compare this murder with the other two murders in the play so far.
Consider:
- who was there
- who committed the murders
- the guilt or innocence of the victims.

The Massacre of the Innocents.

At the time of Jesus's birth there was a king, called Herod, who did not want Jesus to live because he thought he was a threat to his own throne. He sent out a hit gang of soldiers to slaughter all the little boys under the age of 2 years, hoping that Jesus would be among them. Jesus was not, but it did not save those children's lives. This massacre is known as the Slaughter of the Innocents. Herod's motivations for these murders were very much like Macbeth's: nervousness about keeping his throne and suspicion of plots against him.

Context **Discussion**

There have many instances where a member of a family or a close friend has been harmed or threatened in revenge for the actions of a person who is absent.

Members of families and loved friends have also been held as hostages to ensure the return or good behaviour of someone close to them.

Find out about any occurrences of this kind that have happened to people you know or to people in the news.

Report your findings back to the group.

Act 4: Scene 3 Student Activities **35**

Good king, bad king

It is difficult to make this scene dramatically interesting. However, it is an important scene because it allows the play to discuss what it means to be a good king and what makes a bad king.

 **Interpretation**

List the **8** faults of a **bad king** as Malcolm describes them in *Macbeth* (lines 57–60).

- _____
- _____
- _____
- _____
- _____
- _____
- _____
- _____

Which **2** major vices does Malcolm say he himself has in particular?

- _____
- _____

List the **12** virtues of a **good king** as Malcolm describes them (lines 92–4)

- _____
- _____
- _____
- _____
- _____
- _____
- _____
- _____
- _____
- _____
- _____
- _____

Act 4: Scene 3

Context — Discussion

- What qualities would a good king or queen have these days? Do not get sidetracked into a discussion of whether a country should have a monarch. Assume for the purposes of this activity that there is no choice.

- Deception plays a big part in this scene. Malcolm deceives Macduff supposedly in order to test him. Macduff reveals that his morals are not quite as saintly as they could be. Perhaps foul is fair and fair is foul in the characters of these two men also. Look at what Macduff implies about women in Scotland, for example. Or are they simply being realistic about human nature?

Staging

This scene is often cut for performance. Do you think this is justified? If you do think so, use a photocopy of the scene and indicate which lines, words, or speeches you could remove without damaging the sense. Write a short paragraph giving reasons for your cuts. Do not justify every little cut. Make broad, general comments.

_____
_____
_____
_____
_____
_____
_____
_____
_____
_____
_____
_____
_____
_____
_____
_____
_____
_____

Act 4: Scene 3   Student Activities 36

The king's touch

Holinshed writes in his *Chronicles of Scotland* of Edward the Confessor that,

> As hath beene thought he was inspired with the gift of prophesie and also to have had the gift of healing infirmities and diseases. He used to help those that were vexed with the disease, commonlie called the king's evill, and left that viertue as it were a portion of inheritance unto his successors the kings of this realme.

This is a great compliment to James I, as he was a successor to Edward the Confessor on the English throne. It was believed that a good king could, by his touch alone, heal scrofula, a disease of the skin. It was also believed that James did have this gift, passed down to him by the previous kings of England.

There is, however, good dramatic reason for including this snippet of information.

In 1603 James I said that his healing 'touch' was given to him through prayer. He gave the people he touched a medal to hang round their neck as a sign that they had been given the cure. This medal is not mentioned in Holinshed's account but it has been thought that Shakespeare was asked to put this into his play to encourage James to continue this tradition.

The power of belief has been known to produce amazing cures. Holy shrines in many religions and cultures have performed miracles, though whether this is because people believed that they would or for some other reason is not known.

Belief in a supernatural power is important in this play. Macbeth believes in the witches' prophecies for his future. The people of England in the play believe in the healing touch of their king.

French royalty had the power to heal.

Contrast

- The good supernatural story is a contrast with the bad supernatural stories of the witches.
- The story about curing and health is a contrast with the diseased idea of Lady Macbeth's desire to turn her milk to gall.
- In the next act, Macbeth refers to Scotland as his diseased land and asks a doctor if he can cure it.
- There is an obvious contrast between the good, holy king of England and the wicked and unholy king of Scotland.

Act 4: Scene 3 — *Student Activities 36, continued*

 **Discussion**

Research different accounts of healing which seem to be by supernatural powers. Narrate them to the group.

Discuss the idea that healing can depend very much on a person's state of mind.

Charles II touching the heads of his subjects.

Act 4: Scene 3 *Student Activities* **37**

Bad news

Macduff's emotions in this scene suffer agonising and confusing extremes.
- **irritation** *(lines 1–24)* at Malcolm's placid acceptance of Macbeth's evil.
- **despair** *(lines 24–37)* at the loss of his hopes of Malcolm's support.
- **incredulity** *(lines 38–114)* at Malcolm's account of his awful vices.
- **confusion** *(lines 138–9)* at hearing Malcolm reverse his confessions.
- **encouragement** *(lines 140–59)*, possibly, on hearing of the English king's help.
- **pleasure** *(lines 161–76)* at seeing a fellow Scot and relative.
- **nervousness** *(lines 177–200)* as Ross does not fully tell him his terrible news.
- **terrible pain** *(lines 201–24)* as he hears the news of the slaughter.
- **guilt** *(lines 225–7)* as he recognises his part in their murder.
- **vengeful anger** *(lines 232–4)* as he prepares to murder Macbeth.

Before this scene, the play has not given us much idea of Malcolm or Macduff. The main interest of the play has been with Macbeth, Lady Macbeth, Banquo and Duncan.

We have just seen Macduff's wife and son murdered in front of our eyes. There is, therefore, dramatic irony in the scene, as the audience knows what Malcolm and Macduff do not.

The playwright needs to maintain audience interest during a rather long-winded scene discussing the vices and virtues of kings in general between two characters we have hardly seen before in the play.

Structure

Make **notes only** on the following two activities:
- From Ross's entry *(line 159)* to when he tells Macduff about his family *(line 204)*, Ross is gradually preparing Macduff to hear the bad news. How does he do this? Look at his topics of conversation and the language he uses.
- What techniques does Shakespeare use to keep up audience interest in this scene? Look at emotions, language, the sequence of events, etc.

Interpretation Discussion

- What, in your view, is the best way to tell bad news?
- Do you feel sympathy for Macduff in this scene?
- What do you think Lady Macbeth is doing all this time?

Act 5: Scene 1   *Student Activities* **38**

Sleep-walking and sleep-talking

You lack the season of all natures, sleep *(Act 3 Scene 3, line 140)*

These are the last waking words we hear from Lady Macbeth. They were spoken a long time ago in Act 3, just after the disastrous banquet, when she discovered that she and Macbeth could no longer keep up the pretence of innocence. She was speaking to Macbeth but ironically, although he could not sleep, she is the one whose sleep is tortured by guilt and fear of discovery.

What has she been doing in the time between that scene and this? It was made clear to her, as to all the other thanes, that Macbeth had arranged Banquo's murder. She knows about Lady Macduff's murder. She says she could dash out a child's brains herself, but it is Macbeth who arranges for it to be done. After Duncan's murder, Macbeth felt he would never clean his hands of the blood of guilt, but it is she who shows her hands stained with murder.

The secrets of her conscience and heart are, she thinks, written on a private paper and locked in her closet, to which she alone has the key. What she knows and dare not say bubbles out in her sleep. Macbeth expressed his worries by seeing visions. He declared his guilt in the banquet scene and so has nothing much left to hide. But she has to hide all.

Her husband has not been able to rely on her.
- She could not kill Duncan because he looked like her father.
- She has to get drunk before the murder and thinks this will steady her nerves.
- She faints when the body is dicovered.
- Macbeth does not tell her of his plans for Banquo's murder.
- Now she talks in her sleep.

The scene shows her repenting her crimes. A white robe and a burning taper, held to light the confession of crime, was a customary form of shaming for someone repenting. She tries to rub out the damned spot, which represents her guilt. She could also be trying to get rid of traces of being a witch or trying to be a witch. Witches were detected by unusual marks on the body, such as a mole or blemish, which was supposedly the 'nipple' where the familiars sucked. People accused of witchcraft would try to get rid of any marks on the body.

Lady Macbeth has not committed any murder, however. Her greatest violence is in her words.

Either discuss **or** write about the following:
Do you have any sympathy for Lady Macbeth?

Act 5: Scene 1   *Student Activities 38,* continued

Write down what is written on the paper Lady Macbeth locks in her closet.

 **Discussion**

Have you come across any incidents of sleep-walking in your experience or in books?

Have you ever heard anyone talk in their sleep?

Do you think dreams tell us things about what we are trying to hide from ourselves or from others?

A girl is found sleep-walking in a street in California.

Act 5: Scene 5   Student Activities **39**

Blank verse (3): *tomorrow and tomorrow*

Macbeth has just heard of his wife's death and for all their wickedness they do seem to love each other and have a very close relationship. This speech of utter despair – when Macbeth speaks of the pointlessness of existence, the brevity of life, the futility of all our actions on earth and the useless noise that is made by our ranting and our passions – is all the more poignant because of the meaningful sound and rhythm of its poetry. Whatever crimes against humanity he has committed, and these are many and terrible, he is suffering for it now. He is experiencing the loss of any hope or joy or meaning.

Read lines 19–20. Listen to the repetitions of words and letters. What effect do they have? What effect do the words **Creeps** and **petty** have? Do you read the lines quickly or slowly? Line 19 is an unusual blank verse line. It has the normal 5 beats, if you read it as a straightforward blank verse metre:

> To**mo**rrow, **and** to**mo**rrow, and to**mo**rrow

but the line can also be read with three major beats, which sounds more natural:

> **To**morrow, and **to**morrow, and **to**morrow.

In line 20, the alliteration of **petty pace** and **day to day** accentuates the strong beats in the line.

Read line 21. He is speaking of his death and he feels it will be the death of everything. The line has 4 beats. Highlight the words or parts of words below which sound the 4 beats.

> **To the last syllable of recorded time**

Does the fact that there are only 4 beats in this line add to the meaning of the line?

Read lines 22–3. Do you get a mind picture from the imagery in these lines? There is an antithesis between light and dust. In the 16th century, in the country at any rate, people would dip a piece of string in the grease from the evening meal and carry it, lit, as a small light for showing the way up to bed. It only lasted long enough for them to get upstairs, undressed and into bed.

Line 23, contrasted with line 21, is best read with lots of beats, more than the usual five. Highlight the beats you find in the line:

> **The way to dusty death. Out, out, brief candle.**

Does this extra burden of beats have an effect which helps the meaning in any way?

Act 5: Scene 5   *Student Activities 39, continued*

Read lines 24–5. The word **shadow** recalls Psalm 23 'Yeah, though I walk in the valley of the shadow of death'. Macbeth is in the shadow of death now. It also recalls ghosts. It goes on to suggest that an actor is like a shadow. It was a common idea that actors and scenes on the stage were unreal reflections of reality, like shadows.

Line 24 again has an unusual rhythm. The first beat comes on the first word in the line, **Life**. Highlight the beats as you find them in this line.

> **Life's but a walking shadow; a poor player**

Line 25, however, describes the ordinary actor, who thinks he is somebody, striding around the stage, speaking his lines with great energy and meaning. The beats in the line are completely regular: a 5-beat line in straightforward te-tum rhythm. Highlight the beats below.

> **That struts and frets his hour upon the stage.**

Read lines 26–8. Describe the mind picture these lines give. Why is the last line only half a line?

Macbeth End of Play Activities

Your own blank verse speeches

In groups or individually, write a speech, in blank verse, of about 12 lines in length.
Remember: 5-beat lines, usually ten syllables (or eleven or nine) and non-rhyming. You could rhyme the last two lines to create a rhyming couplet to give an effect of ending.
Choose one of the following characters in the situations suggested.

- Malcolm at the end of Act 1 Scene 4. This is a soliloquy. He has just heard that his father has made him Prince of Cumberland. Suggest the mixed feelings this gives him. He has not been very successful in the battle. He compares himself with Macbeth perhaps. He may realise that Macbeth could have expected to be made king after Duncan's death. Does he express any love for his father? Does he feel excited about the prospect of being king eventually?

- Lady Macbeth at the end of Act 1 Scene 5. She is preparing for Duncan's arrival with his soldiers and thanes. She speaks with some servants telling them what to prepare. Include little domestic details of food and beds and so on. Do not forget that later in the play she drugs the guards' drinks. You could perhaps give her a couple of asides, spoken to herself, in which she gives hints of what else she is thinking about.

- Banquo at the end of Act 2, after the coronation of Macbeth at Scone and before he speaks with Macbeth at the beginning of Act 3. This is a soliloquy. He remembers how wonderful Macbeth was in battle. Add details here of bloody events in the fighting. He could be full of admiration for him on one level. Include his feelings about Duncan. Did he like him as a king and as a man? What did he feel about his death? Banquo would also have something to say about the witches. If you can fit it in, mention what he thinks of the thanes who did not go to the coronation.

- Macbeth at the end of Act 3 Scene 4. He has just seen Banquo's ghost at the banquet and been comforted by Lady Macbeth. Continue Macbeth's words to Lady Macbeth. He is telling her what he is going to do next. He is finding comfort in the thought that he can do something positive to secure his safety on the throne. You may include a line or two from Lady Macbeth, but it should be largely his words and thoughts. He thinks about the thanes he has just seen. Give details of what he plans to do to them.

- Fleance when he hears about the murder of Macduff's family. You can make him quite young and so his language could be fairly simple, although it must be in blank verse. Fleance remembers the night of his father's murder and his own terrifying escape. He could describe it in some detail. Does he feel sympathy for the young son of Macduff? Perhaps he knew him and his brothers and sisters. He could mention the night when he and his father met Macbeth just before the murder of Duncan. Is he now frightened of the dark?

- Macduff at the very end of the play. He thinks with elation about killing Macbeth. It had been a long time coming after he had heard about his family's murder. He would be very satisfied. Also he would be very sad. Now that revenge is achieved he may feel empty. He no longer has revenge to plan for and his family are all dead. He could remember their good qualities.

Character collage, programme notes, modern version

Character collage

Choose one character from the play.

- Take a poster-sized piece of paper.
- Cut out from newspapers, magazines, packaging, photos, junk mail, pictures or lettering anything which strikes you as connected, in some way, with your chosen character.
- Arrange the poster to create an image of the character. It can recall aspects of personality, job, looks, relationship, action or all of these.
- Display it.

Programme notes

Choose an audience group from among the following:

- 10-year-old children. They do not know the play or the story.
- A business persons' conference. An experience in how not to do things!
- French teenagers. They are on an advanced English-language course.
- Students on a psychology course. An experience in the subtleties of influence.
- People in any institution or organisation – for example, staff from a supermarket, bank or factory, or people in a prison, passengers on a cruise.
- Any other audience group you would like to choose.

Decide on a special way to present the play for this audience group. Give your production an angle that would be especially interesting to them.

Write the programme notes for your imaginary production. You will need to include:

- An introduction telling a little of the story but not too much. Even people who have read or seen the play, cannot necessarily remember the details. Grab their interest.
- A few short quotations from the play, again to get interest going.
- A paragraph explaining something their group will find interesting in the play.
- Some quotations from other writers (or from imaginary people in the company or institution the audience belongs to).

Finally, if you wish, or have time, illustrate your notes and present them as a programme.

Macbeth — End of Play Activities 41, *continued*

Modern version of a scene

Choose part of the play which is about 100 lines long. It does not have to be a whole scene – you could choose two parts of two different scenes, of around 50 lines each, and put them together.

- Read the passage through several times until you are familiar with it.
- Decide how the situation in the scene could be interpreted in modern life.
- Write a completely modern English version.
    - Do not try to use Shakespearian language.
    - Keep the new scene about the same length as the original.
    - Keep roughly the same number of characters, although you may need an added part.
    - Use modern names for people and let them talk about modern things.
- Learn your modern version and present it to an audience, or video it for your own viewing.
- If you have time, present the original version also, after the modern one.

Alternative views – discussion

In defence of the witches

The hierarchical society of the play can be seen as deceptive, oppressive and constantly at war.
- The witches are themselves outsiders from this system, living in a community with others like themselves.
- They expose the rotten motives beneath the heroic in bringing out Macbeth's ambitions.
- Their words are true. It is only Macbeth who interprets them to bring about his wishes.
- Meanings are not fixed in their world – 'Fair is foul and foul is fair.' We cannot tell if they are men or women and even their bodies melt into air. Finally Macbeth himself is uncertain of all meaning – 'Life's but a walking shadow'.
- They do no actual physical harm themselves. The witches work and live together in a group whereas Macbeth and his wife are out for their own ends.
- It is possible that social order in a country can only change by dissolving existing fixed ideas, relationships and meanings.

Masculinity and femininity

The images of male and female in *Macbeth* are very disturbed.
- The image of powerful manhood at the beginning is of a butcher in the battlefield. Manhood is equated with killing.
- Duncan is a father and mother figure, giving lineage and honour but also connected with images of nurturing. He is ineffectual as his kingdom is attacked and has rebels and he is feebly overtrusting. Does the weak female unleash female chaos?
- The witches are sexually ambiguous.
- Lady Macbeth evinces very unwomanly desires to turn her milk to gall and dash out a baby's brains.
- Duncan's body is described as a 'new Gorgon', which is female.
- Witches were popularly thought to suckle with poison and the poisoned cauldron is the opposite of nurturing. The good mother, Lady Macduff, is murdered.
- Does the play show fears of female power?
- Many points in the play discuss what it is to be a man, eg Macbeth and Lady Macbeth Acts 1 and 3, Macduff Act 4.
- The family tree is strictly patriarchal. Male power is finally restored.

Uses and abuses of the text

 **Language**

From anywhere in the text of *Macbeth*, find a quotation that you think would be appropriate or amusing for each of the following purposes:
- a Christmas card
- a New Year's card
- a birthday card
- a Mother's Day card
- a Father's Day card
- as a thank-you note.

Find a quotation from anywhere in the text of the play that you could laminate and put up in each of the following places:
- the dentist's waiting-room
- the doctor's waiting-room
- a school dining-room
- on the lid or door of your desk or locker
- in the library
- on your own bedroom wall.

Find a short quotation that would be appropriate or amusing to paint or print on to each of the following (and do not do this without express permission from the owner!):
- a pair of trainers
- a bag
- a teatowel
- a bedsheet
- a pillowcase
- a shower curtain.

Find a quotation which would be appropriate for any of the following:
- a newspaper heading for an item of news you have heard or read this week
- an advertising slogan for selling ice-cream (or something else)
- a title for a brand-new comedy show for TV
- the name of a pop group.

Macbeth (1)

It will have blood, they say; blood will have blood (Act 3 Scene 4, line 121)

Act 1 Scene 2

Macbeth excels as a soldier and a faithful general. Find quotations describing him and his actions.

Act 1 Scene 3

What is the suggestion that Macbeth yields to when he hears the prophecies? What does he feel about these thoughts? Use one- or two-word quotes to support your view.

How does he explain being wrapped up in his thoughts to the other thanes who are present? What does this indicate to you about his state of mind?

Act 1 Scene 4

What two opposite impressions does he give, to Duncan and to the audience?

Act 1 Scene 5

What impression of Macbeth do we get from Lady Macbeth's comments on him? How does he seem with her when he enters?

Macbeth (2)

Character Sheet 45

Act 1 Scene 7

Why did Macbeth not greet Duncan when he arrived, and why has he now left the feast and gone antisocially into an ante-chamber?

_____
_____
_____

Find **six** aspects of his character shown in the first speech of the scene. Consider intelligence, knowledge, insight, energy, fullness of language, guilt … or others. Find a short quote for each.

_____
_____
_____

When does he decide not to kill Duncan? Do you think he wanted to be persuaded?

_____
_____
_____

Act 2 Scene 1

Is he trying to involve Banquo? What effect does the vision have on him?

_____
_____
_____

Act 2 Scene 2

How is Macbeth's reaction to murder different from his wife's? Does he regret it?

_____
_____
_____

Act 2 Scene 3

Macbeth's comments are very short to begin with. By line 89 he is able to speak. What do the double meanings in his words show about his change of heart?

_____
_____
_____

Macbeth   *Character Sheet* **46**

Macbeth (3)

Act 3 Scene 1
Macbeth, now king, is seen after time has passed. How does he behave to Banquo and the murderers?

Act 3 Scene 2
He is much more determined about this murder than he was before Duncan's. Pick a few lines which demonstrate this.

Act 3 Scene 4
Why can he not forget Banquo and enjoy the feast? Pick out the words he says just before the ghost enters. What do they suggest about the ghost?

How does he react to his fear in this scene when the guests have gone?

Act 4 Scene 1
Macbeth practises necromancy, or conjuring, to find out his future. Pick out the words of command he uses with the spirits.

Act 4 Scene 3
We do not see Macbeth for the rest of the act but he is very present in the thoughts of Macduff, Malcolm and therefore the audience. List the descriptions of him given by Macduff and Malcolm.

Macbeth   *Character Sheet* **47**

Macbeth (4)

Act 5 Scene 3

We have not seen Macbeth for four long scenes. His moods are swinging from one feeling to another. Find your own words to describe these different moods.

Act 5 Scene 5

Did Macbeth love his wife? What does his reaction to her death show?

He is also abandoned by the witches, as it seems to him. How does he react to this? Find the quote which shows he has lost faith.

Act 5 Scene 7

Macbeth does recognise his guilt in the murder of Macduff's family, even though he did not do it himself. Find the quote.

Find the quote which shows he does not believe the witches any more.

How do you interpret his mood just before he dies? Does this show any good side to his character at the end?

Macbeth Character Sheet **48**

Banquo (1)

> True worthy Banquo; he is full so valiant,
> And in his commendations I am fed
> *(Act 1 Scene 4, lines 54–5)*

Act 1 Scene 2

Banquo is praised alongside Macbeth. Find a quotation to show this.

_____

_____

Act 1 Scene 3

Describe **three** of his reactions to the witches.

_____

_____

_____

_____

Find a quotation which links him with natural growth.

_____

Act 1 Scene 4

How does his only line in this scene add to our image of him?

_____

_____

Act 1 Scene 6

Here Banquo is linked with ideas of breeding and religion. Find short quotes to support this view.

_____

_____

Act 2 Scene 1

How are the ideas of healthy breeding and heaven continued in the opening of this scene?

_____

_____

How does Banquo relate with Macbeth here? Why does he bring up the topic of the witches?

_____

Macbeth
Banquo (2)

Character Sheet 49

Act 2 Scene 3

Banquo only speaks twice in this scene. What do his speeches show us about his reactions? He is silent much of the time. How do you think he would react physically?

Act 3 Scene 1

Banquo is the first person we see after Macbeth becomes king. What are his thoughts about Macbeth's actions? He does not say anything. Should he have?
Is he hoping his children will be kings? Find evidence.

In his soliloquy *(lines 49–53)* Macbeth praises Banquo highly. In your own words, what qualities does he say Banquo has?

When Macbeth speaks to the murderers, what does he suggest about Banquo? Do you believe him?

Do you think Banquo suspected his time had come?

Macbeth Character Sheet **50**

Duncan (1)

> this Duncan
> Hath borne his faculties so meek, hath been
> So clear in his great office *(Act 1 Scene 7, lines 16–18)*

Act 1 Scene 2
What is Duncan's role in this scene?

Act 1 Scene 4
How does Duncan greet Macbeth and Banquo? What can you tell about his thoughts from the language he uses? Find quotes to support this.

Why does he make his son Prince of Cumberland at this moment?

Act 1 Scene 6
Duncan is greeted at the castle with the pomp due to a king. How many times does he use the word **love**?

Act 1 Scene 7
What does Macbeth say about Duncan?

Act 2 Scene 1
How does Banquo describe the king's mood and actions at the feast?

Act 2 Scene 2
Lady Macbeth says Duncan resembled her father. How old do you think he is?

Macbeth

Duncan (2)

Character Sheet 51

Act 2 Scene 3

Lennox describes an unruly night. What do these disturbances of the weather add to our impression of Duncan's status?

_____

_____

_____

_____

Macduff refers to Duncan as **The Lord's anointed temple**. What does this mean, and how does it add to the seriousness of his murder?

_____

_____

_____

_____

Macbeth's description of the murdered body also gives Duncan status. Quote it.

_____

_____

_____

_____

Act 2 Scene 4

The Old Man's account of the night adds to Duncan's status. How?

_____

_____

_____

_____

_____

Macbeth Character Sheet **52**

Lady Macbeth (1)

I may pour my spirits in thine ear,
And chastise with the valour of my tongue
(Act 1 Scene 5, lines 25–6)

Act 1 Scene 5

What does the letter tell us of Macbeth's feelings about his wife?

_____

_____

Read Lady Macbeth's first two lines out loud. What tones of voice do you hear, and what first impression of her do you get?

_____

_____

_____

From the rest of the soliloquy *(lines 17–29)*, what is suggested about her view of her husband, and what does this suggest about her?

_____

_____

_____

Her prayer to evil spirits links her with the witches and her character comes across powerfully. Does she have to make herself like a man in order to fulfil her ambition?

_____

_____

Her welcome of her husband is emotional. How would you describe the way she relates to him? Pick out two short quotes which indicate this.

_____

_____

Act 1 Scene 6

At the end of Scene 5 she says, **Leave all the rest to me.** She takes control, welcoming Duncan to the castle where she knows he is going to be murdered. What do the words **twice done, and then done double** suggest about her here?

Eye of Newt and toe of Starr, some DNA and a cigar…

_____

_____

Nelson Thornes Shakespeare: *Macbeth* © Dinah Jurksaitis, Nelson Thornes Ltd, 2003

Macbeth Character Sheet 53

Lady Macbeth (2)

Act 1 Scene 7

How does Lady Macbeth demonstrate her strength when dealing with her husband's hesitations?

List her methods.

___

Act 2 Scene 2

Lady Macbeth begins the scene in a state of nervousness. How is this shown?

___

When she finds that no one has discovered her husband at the scene of the crime, she takes control again. What is her attitude now to his fears? How does she show her practical common sense?

___

Act 2 Scene 3

What is her reaction when the murder of Duncan is discovered by the others? What does this show about her?

___

Act 3 Scene 2

She is now queen, but speaks of her unhappiness. Why is she unhappy? Consider her guilt and fear and loss of intimacy with her husband.

Macbeth Character Sheet 54

Lady Macbeth (3)

Act 3 Scene 4
Lady Macbeth attempts to be the perfect hostess. How?

_____
_____

How does Lady Macbeth react to Macbeth's visions, both towards him and towards the guests?

_____
_____
_____
_____

After the guests have gone, she changes in her tone towards Macbeth. How is she now?

_____
_____
_____

Her last waking words are: **You lack the season of all natures, sleep**.
How is this comment ironic considering when we next see her?

Act 5 Scene 1
She has been absent from the stage for five long scenes. She has lost her mind and is sleep-walking. What does she reveal to the waiting-woman and doctor?

_____
_____
_____
_____

Do you have any sympathy for her?

_____
_____

Macbeth

GCSE Coursework Assignment

> Tomorrow, and tomorrow, and tomorrow,
> Creeps in this petty pace from day to day
>> (Act 5 Scene 5, lines 19–20)

Even though Macbeth is clearly a villain, our responses to him are not one-sided. How does Shakespeare create a mixed response to Macbeth at various moments in the play?

Write about these points:

- the language used about Macbeth at the beginning of the play when he has saved Scotland
- the effect the meeting with the witches has on his thoughts and actions
- the influence Lady Macbeth and his own imagination have on his actions
- how you could dramatise the despair and loss he feels at the end of the play.

Assignment guidance

As you read through the play, prepare the coursework by considering some of the following questions.

Is it possible in **Act 1** to see the good in Macbeth and any justification for his feeling that he should be king? Consider:

- descriptions of him in battle
- his reaction to Malcolm becoming Prince of Cumberland
- his reaction to the witches' prophecy and later to his wife's persuasions
- Macbeth's concerns and doubts about the murder he is planning.

In **Act 2** how does he feel about the murder, just before and then after he has done it? Consider:

- his bad conscience, compared with his wife's reactions
- his way of speaking when the body is discovered. Does he lie?

In **Act 3** as he gets deeper into murder, do you feel sympathy for him or only revulsion? Consider:

- his persuasion of the murderers
- his seeing the ghost of Banquo and his reactions to it
- the effect his reign has had on his thanes.

In **Act 4** is he completely under the influence of the witches or could he still, in your opinion, have the power to resist them? Consider:
- his meeting with the witches
- the way he orders the murder of Macduff's family
- what we learn about his actions from the three men in Scene 3.

In **Act 5**, now that he has committed so many atrocities, is there still any possibility of sympathy for him? Consider:
- his wife's madness and his feelings for her
- his confidence in the witches
- his despair.

To help with this assignment, you may like to use some of the following:

Activity Sheet Title	*Number*	*Act/Scene*
Macbeth character sheets	44–7	
Clothing imagery	7	Act 1 Scene 3
Obsession	23	Act 3 Scene 1
Sleep and nightmares	25	Act 3 Scene 2
Compare with the murder of Duncan	26	Act 3 Scene 3

Macbeth

GCSE Coursework Assignment

> Here's the smell of the blood still. All the prefumes of
> Arabia will not sweeten this little hand. Oh, oh, oh
>
> *(Act 5 Scene 1, lines 50–2)*

Do you think that Lady Macbeth, despite her words, can still be pitied? Write about Shakespeare's presentation of the different sides of her character.

Write about these points:
- how Lady Macbeth prepares herself to meet her husband after she has read his letter
- what methods and language she uses to persuade her husband to kill Duncan
- in what ways she supports her husband after the murder has been committed
- how you could dramatise the last view we have of her sleep-walking.

Assignment guidance

As you read through the play prepare the coursework by considering some of the following questions.

How in **Act 1** does Lady Macbeth appear to you? Consider:
- her feelings about her husband and her knowledge of him
- her prayer to evil spirits
- the language and manner she uses with her husband.
- does she give the impression that she will take part in the murder?

In **Act 2** we experience the murder, as it is happening, through Lady Macbeth's excitement, fear and nervousness. Afterwards she only plays a small part in this act. What do you feel about her here? Consider:
- how you are affected by her words at the beginning of Scene 2
- how she and Macbeth speak together in this scene
- her actions with the daggers and blood and her comments about her father
- her reaction to the discovery of the murder.

In **Act 3** she is now queen. Has she changed? Consider:
- her words to her husband in Scene 2 and his manner towards her
- her behaviour as hostess to her guests
- her words to her husband when he is seeing the ghost
- her attitude towards him after the banquet. Has it changed?

Take **Act 4** and **Act 5** together. What do you think Lady Macbeth is doing while Macbeth visits the witches, orders the murders of Macduff's family and prepares for war against the English and the thanes?

Macbeth — GCSE Coursework Assignment 2, continued

Act 5 is one of the most memorable scenes in Shakespeare's plays. Words from it are known the world over. Describe your response to her in this act. Consider:
- is she mad or just simply sleep-talking?
- what is the paper she folds? Has she got a conscience?
- has she committed any atrocities? Is she wicked?

To help with this assignment, you may like to use the following:

Activity Sheet Title	Number	Act/Scene
Lady Macbeth character sheets	52–4	
Lady Macbeth	11	Act 1 Scene 5
Relationship and euphemism	14	Act 1 Scene 7
Things change	28	Act 3 Scene 4
Sleep-walking and sleep-talking	38	Act 5 Scene 1

Macbeth

GCSE Coursework Assignment

> And be these juggling fiends no more believed,
> That palter with us in a double sense
>
> *(Act 5 Scene 8, lines 19–20)*

Discuss the importance of the supernatural in *Macbeth*. How does Shakespeare use it to create dramatic interest? Give your own version of how the witches, their apparitions and the ghost could be shown on stage or film to reflect uncanny happenings in today's world.

An appropriate plan for the coursework assignment could be:

1. to explore the reasons why the witches are so important in the story and as an effect on stage or film
2. to summarise briefly how Shakespeare's audience would have felt about witches and why
3. to give an outline of your version of the dramatic presentation of the witches, the apparitions and the ghost, explaining why you have chosen these interpretations
4. to describe in detail either one scene or several scenes, highlighting the presence of the witches, ghost or apparitions as you have interpreted them.

Include analysis and quotations.

Assignment guidance

As you read through the play prepare the coursework by considering some of the following questions.

In **Act 1** consider first how you would present the witches and if you would show them at times when they are not speaking. Then consider:

- which speeches/words of Macbeth and Lady Macbeth show the witches' influence
- how to use sound, colour or gesture to connect the witches and the Macbeths.

In **Act 2**, darkness, tolling bells, bird sounds, feasting and drinking, a dead body and visions could all maintain the feeling of the supernatural. How?

- Consider how or whether you would use the Porter and Old Man to develop your ideas. Could the witches have a comic side to them?

In **Act 3** the witches do not speak until Scene 5. How could you make an audience remain aware of them in a production? Consider:

- the murderers: there are three of them eventually
- the ghost and its effect on Macbeth
- how you would present the larger group of witches in Scene 5.

Macbeth — GCSE Coursework Assignment 3, continued

Act 4 Scene 1 offers a wealth of opportunity in the presentation of the apparitions. Consider:

- how you can interpret the meanings of the apparitions in their dramatic presentation
- Lady Macbeth is not seen at all in this act. Would you have her watching any of it or appearing in some other way?

In **Act 5** how have Lady Macbeth and Macbeth been influenced by the witches in the way they walk, talk or what they do on stage? Consider:

- the sleep-walking and the death of Lady Macbeth
- Macbeth's behaviour with his soldiers and servants.

To help with this assignment, you may like to use the following:

Activity Sheet Title	Number	Act/Scene
Introductory essay: Witches		
Performance interpretation: witches (1)	4	Act 1 Scene 3
Echoing … choing … oing … ing … g	8	Act 1 Scenes 1–3
Sound and guilt	15	Act 2 Scene 2
Sleep and nightmares	25	Act 3 Scene 2
Performance interpretation: the ghost	27	Act 3 Scene 4
Performance interpretation: witches (2)	30	Act 4 Scene 1
Spells and visions	31	Act 4 Scene 1

Macbeth

GCSE Coursework Assignment

> look like the innocent flower,
> But be the serpent under't
>
> *(Act 1 Scene 5, lines 64–5)*

Show how deception is an important aspect of *Macbeth*.

Consider:

- how deception is related to events at the time the play was written
- how the witches, Lady Macbeth and Macbeth use deception
- possible ways of interpreting one or two scenes in order to show deception.

An appropriate plan for the coursework assignment could be:

1. to explain briefly how deception was a part of the Gunpowder Plot and the circumstances surrounding it
2. to explore how the witches deceive Macbeth and how this is discovered by him at the end of the play
3. to discuss how Macbeth attempts to deceive the thanes after the murder and how Lady Macbeth tries to cover up their crime
4. to describe ways in which you could use stage or film to emphasise this side of the play.

Include analysis and quotations.

Assignment guidance

As you read through the play prepare the coursework by considering some of the following questions.

Macbeth begins deception early. Where in **Act 1** do we see this? Does he struggle against it? Consider:

- his rapt reaction to the witches' prophecy and his excuse for it
- if, in your opinion, he knows about the Thane of Cawdor's treachery
- his language with Duncan when he returns from the battle
- his inability to greet Duncan when he arrives at Macbeth's castle
- his absence from the banquet.

In **Act 2** Macbeth's deception is effective after the murder. How does he equivocate with the sons and thanes? Does he get better at deception?

- Look in particular at Scene 3 from line 43 to line 132. This is a major part of the assignment.

In **Act 3** Macbeth has become king. Look at how

- he deceives in his conversation with Banquo and with the murderers
- his lies are exposed in the banquet scene when he sees the ghost and reacts to it and what this indicates about conscience.

Macbeth — GCSE Coursework Assignment 4, *continued*

Take **Act 4** and **Act 5** together. How is Macbeth deceived into false confidence by the apparitions the witches show him? Take each apparition in turn and look at:
- what the witches intended Macbeth to understand
- what the truth turned out to be.

To help with this assignment, you may like to use the following:

Activity Sheet Title	Number	Act/Scene
Introductory essay: The Gunpowder Plot and equivocation		
Clothing imagery	7	Act 1 Scene 3
Dramatic irony and diplomatic talk	9	Act 1 Scene 4
Night and day	10	Act 1 Scene 5
Contrast and double	12	Act 1 Scene 6
The Porter's speech	18	Act 2 Scene 3
Equivocation	19	Act 2 Scene 3
Equivocation in Act 2 Scene 3	20	Act 2 Scene 3
Sleep-walking and sleep-talking	38	Act 5 Scene 1

Macbeth

AS Level Coursework Assignment

> So from that spring whence comfort seemed to come
> Discomfort swells
>
> *(Act 1 Scene 2, lines 27–8)*

'Fair is foul, and foul is fair.' Discuss this comment in the light of the play *Macbeth*.

Consider:

- what supports this comment in the politics of the time the play was written and in present times
- an analysis of how the idea is developed in the play and different ways of presenting any of the following characters in relation to the comment: Macbeth, Lady Macbeth, the witches
- can the witches be seen as 'the heroines of the piece'?
- a discussion of the killings in the play. Are they justified by the circumstances?

An appropriate plan for the coursework assignment could be:

1. to give a brief discussion of how the religious changes in England had led to what had previously been accepted as good, becoming seen as bad
2. to discuss briefly how this may be seen in thinking and being in today's world
3. to examine how the perception of Macbeth changes during the play from a hero who saved Scotland to a murderous tyrannical ruler
4. to examine the hidden evil and show of good of Macbeth and Lady Macbeth and to offer a variety of ways of presenting this aspect of them and of the witches
5. to read Terry Eagleton's essay 'The witches are the heroines of the piece' and show how these foul women can be seen as fair!
6. to show how fair is foul and foul is fair with reference to the killings in the play. Is the final killing of Macbeth justified? Was his killing of the Norwegians justified? Is there ever a just war?

Material to help you with this assignment can be found in:

Activity Sheet Title	Number	Act/Scene
Introductory essay: The Gunpowder Plot and equivocation		
Fair is foul and foul is fair	1	Act 1 Scene 1
The battle	2	Act 1 Scene 2
Dramatic irony and diplomatic talk	9	Act 1 Scene 4
Contrast and double	12	Act 1 Scene 6
Equivocation	19	Act 2 Scene 3
Equivocation in Act 2 Scene 3	20	Act 2 Scene 3
Compare with the murder of Duncan	26	Act 3 Scene 3
Coded language	32	Act 4 Scene 2
Good king, bad king	35	Act 4 Scene 3

Some critical essays on the topic are:

Jonathan Bate and Russell Jackson (eds), *Shakespeare: An Illustrated Stage History* (Oxford University Press: 1996)

Terry Eagleton, 'The witches are the heroines of the piece', in Alan Sinfield (ed), *Macbeth* (New Casebooks series; Macmillan: 1992)

G Wilson-Knight, 'The Milk of Concord: an essay on life-themes in *Macbeth*', in John Wain (ed), *Macbeth* (Casebook series; Macmillan: 1968)

Macbeth

AS Level Coursework Assignment

> Do you not hope your children shall be kings
> (*Act 1 Scene 3, line 118*)

Macbeth explores feelings about inheritance. What are your views on this aspect of the play?

Consider:

- the time the play was written and how this could have influenced concerns about inheritance in the play
- Macbeth and Lady Macbeth's concerns about fertility and the witches' use of this
- imagery of fruitfulness and waste
- various perspectives of whether there is any sympathy to be had for the two main characters in their despair at the end of the play, when they have lost their friends, influence, sense of worth and their souls.

An appropriate plan for the coursework assignment could be:

1. to discuss briefly that James I has recently become king after the childless Elizabeth. He was said to be related to Banquo and also to inherit the king's healing touch.
2. to trace the concerns about progeny that are expressed by Macbeth and Lady Macbeth and give your own views on the importance of this in their actions
3. to compare the Macbeths with Banquo, Duncan, Malcolm and Macduff
4. to discuss the Macbeths' deaths and the despair and loss both feel as they have cut themselves off from community. Explore various views on whether we can have any sympathy for them.

Assignment guidance

As you read through the play prepare the coursework by considering some of the following questions.

How does **Act 1** introduce ideas and images of inheritance? Consider:
- what Macbeth and Banquo are promised and their reactions to this
- Duncan's concern for Malcolm
- Lady Macbeth's prayer to evil forces
- images of fruitfulness and waste.

Take **Act 2** and **Act 3** together.

Act 2 begins with Fleance and ends with Malcolm and Donalbain. Why do you think Shakespeare introduced them at this point?

Macbeth — AS Level Coursework Assignment 6, continued

In **Act 3** Macbeth's obsession with children grows. Discuss in detail
- his soliloquy in Scene 1 line 47
- his conversation with his wife at the end of Scene 2
- the attempted murder of Fleance.

In **Act 4**
- how do the witches play on his obsession in Scene 1?
- how and why does Shakespeare make the murder of the Macduff family moving?
- how does Macduff react to the news of his family's murder?

After reading **Act 5** discuss the following:
- why do you think Macbeth is so concerned with children?
- how do you view Lady Macbeth's rejection of her own fruitfulness?
- do you sympathise with their despair at the end of the play?

Material to help you with this assignment can be found in:

Activity Sheet Title	Number	Act/Scene
Introductory essay: Witches		
Dramatic irony and diplomatic talk	9	Act 1 Scene 4
Lady Macbeth	11	Act 1 Scene 5
Contrast and double	12	Act 1 Scene 6
Relationship and euphemism	14	Act 1 Scene 7
Obsession	23	Act 3 Scene 1
The slaughter of the innocents	34	Act 4 Scene 2
The king's touch	36	Act 4 Scene 3
Bad news	37	Act 4 Scene 3
Sleep-walking and sleep-talking	38	Act 5 Scene 1
Blank verse (3)	39	Act 5 Scene 5

Some critical essays on the topic are:

Janet Adelman, 'Born of woman: fantasies of maternal power in *Macbeth*', in Alan Sinfield (ed), *Macbeth* (New Casebooks series; Macmillan: 1992)

Marilyn French, '*Macbeth* and masculine values' in Alan Sinfield (ed), *Macbeth*

Sigmund Freud, 'The character of Lady Macbeth', in Alan Sinfield (ed) *Macbeth*